CHEMISTRY TODAY SECOND EDITION
Laboratory Manual

R.L. Whitman
Vice-Principal, Queen Elizabeth High School

E.E. Zinck
Dean of Science, Acadia University

R.A. Nalepa
Head of Science Department, Halifax West High School

PRENTICE-HALL CANADA INC., Scarborough, Ontario

Canadian Cataloguing in Publication Data
Whitman, R. L. (Ronald Laurie), 1944-
  Chemistry today. Laboratory manual

Supplement to: Whitman, R. L. (Ronald Laurie), 1944-
Chemistry today.

ISBN 0-13-129551-9

1. Chemistry. I. Zinck, E. E., 1938-
II. Nalepa, R. A. (Robert Allan), 1948-
III. Title.

QD31.2.W572   540   C82-094873-X

Prentice-Hall, Inc., Englewood Cliffs, New Jersey
Prentice-Hall International, Inc., London
Prentice-Hall of Australia, Pty., Ltd., Sydney
Prentice-Hall of India Pvt., Ltd., New Delhi
Prentice-Hall of Japan, Inc., Tokyo
Prentice-Hall of Southeast Asia (Pte.) Ltd., Singapore
Editora Prentice-Hall do Brasil Ltda., Rio de Janeiro

ISBN 0-13-129551-9

Metric Commission Canada has granted use
of the National Symbol for Metric Conversion

2   3   4   5   JD   86   85   84   83

Contents

Introduction

Chemists search for answers to chemical problems in the laboratory. This laboratory manual is designed to permit you to do some of the experiments chemists have done, and to follow their reasoning as they searched for the answers to their questions. As you do the experiments in this manual, you will gain skills in observation, inquiry, and analysis.

How much you gain from the laboratory will depend on you. On one hand, if you simply go through the motions by slavishly following instructions, you will gain very little. On the other hand, if you are interested in what is occurring and why, and ask yourself questions regarding every aspect of each experiment, you will profit much from laboratory work.

As you perform an experiment, you should make a conscientious effort to answer any questions found in the **Procedure** section. The main portion of each laboratory report will normally be made up of answers to the questions found in the experiment, along with data tables and mathematical calculations as required.

A chemistry laboratory is a safe place provided that you pay attention and use your common sense. Certain rules and regulations must be followed in order for you to receive the maximum benefit from your efforts in the laboratory.

SAFETY RULES

I General Safety Procedures

1. Appropriate safety goggles should be worn *at all times* while working in the chemistry laboratory. Prescription eyeglasses do not offer proper protection from spills and splashes.

2. Special care should be taken when wearing contact lenses in the laboratory. If chemicals enter the eyes they may become trapped behind the contact lenses. There is a further difficulty in removing the lenses under such circumstances. Students should advise their instructors if they are wearing contact lenses.

1

3. Never attempt to carry out unauthorized experiments. Your teacher must give approval for all unassigned experiments. *Never work alone* in the laboratory, even during class hours: if you have an accident, there will be no one to help you.

4. Learn the location and proper use of all safety equipment such as fire extinguishers, fire blankets, safety showers, and eye wash fountains.

5. Do not enter chemical storage areas without authorization.

6. Be alert and work carefully at all times in the chemistry laboratory. Take care not to bump into other students. Remain at your laboratory station while performing an experiment. An unattended experiment can produce unwanted results.

7. Do not run, play practical jokes, or engage in horseplay in the laboratory.

8. Do not eat, drink, or smoke in the laboratory.

9. Your laboratory working area should not be cluttered with books or clothing.

10. Report all accidents, even minor ones, to your teacher. Also, if you or someone near you feels faint or dizzy, report it immediately to the teacher.

11. A student who has been splashed with chemicals in the eyes may not be able to open them. Lead the student by the hand to the eye wash fountain and begin to flush the eyes with water. Notify your teacher of the accident. Flush the eyes with plenty of water for at least *fifteen minutes*. If contact lenses are being worn, they must be removed. *Remember:* Speed is essential. Following an eye accident, the victim should be examined by a doctor.

II Handling Chemicals

1. Read the label on a reagent bottle at least twice before removing any of its contents. Do not take the reagent bottle to your desk, and do not take any more material than is required. When you have finished with the bottle, return it immediately to its proper place.

2. Acids, bases, bromine, and other corrosive liquids may burn the skin severely. Wash any chemical spills from the skin with large volumes of running water.

3. Never add water to concentrated acids (especially sulfuric acid). Instead, slowly add the acid to the water, stirring constantly.

4. Do not taste chemicals.

5. When instructed to smell chemicals, never smell them directly. Use your hand to fan the vapours towards your nose. If you are directed to use the fume hood, do so. Never put your head in the fume hood during an experiment.

6. While doing experiments, keep your hands away from your face and eyes. You should wash your hands thoroughly at the end of each laboratory period.

7. Never use your mouth to draw a liquid into a pipet. Use a safety bulb on the pipet.

8. Carry out operations with flammable solvents in flasks rather than in open beakers.

9. All reactions involving hazardous or irritating, volatile chemicals should should be carried out in a fume hood.

10. Liquid mercury and its vapours are hazardous. Open vessels of mercury must never be allowed in the laboratory. Liquid mercury should never come in contact with your skin. Mercury spills must be cleaned up quickly.

III Storage and Disposal

1. Dispose of all chemicals in the containers provided by your teacher.

2. Never return any unused chemicals to their original containers. *This could cause contamination!* Do not place anything in a reagent bottle except the dropper or Scoopula® provided.

3. Clean up all spills immediately. Neutralize acid or alkali spills as directed by your teacher.

4. Discard paper, matches (properly extinguished), and other insoluble solids as directed by your teacher. *Do not throw them into the sink.*

5. Never pour flammable liquids or hot acids into the sink.

6. Do not use glass stoppers for bottles containing alkali solutions. These solutions dissolve glass, causing the stoppers to become stuck in the bottles.

7. At the end of the laboratory period, wash and rinse all glassware and return all equipment to the proper location. Wash and wipe off your desktop and wash your hands. Be sure that the gas and water are turned off.

IV Heating Precautions

1. No flammable liquid should be used in the presence of an open flame. Care should also be taken to ensure that electrical equipment cannot produce a spark.

2. Do not bring any substance in contact with a flame, unless specifically instructed to do so.

3. Never boil a liquid in a closed system. Boiling chips should always be used to facilitate smooth boiling.

4. When heating a liquid in a test tube, make sure the test tube is not pointed at anyone.

5. When heating materials, use only heat resistant glassware.

6. Gas burners should be lighted in accordance with your teacher's instructions.

7. Use extreme caution when using a burner. Never leave a burner flame unattended. Loose clothing should not be worn in the laboratory, and long hair should be tied back to keep it away from the burner flame. If your burner is not operating properly, turn off the gas, and notify your teacher.

8. Be wary of hot glass. Hot glass and cold glass look exactly alike; however, they can be distinguished by bringing the back of your hand near the glass. Bathe skin burns in cold water. If the skin is charred or broken, seek medical help immediately.

Common Equipment Used in This Manual

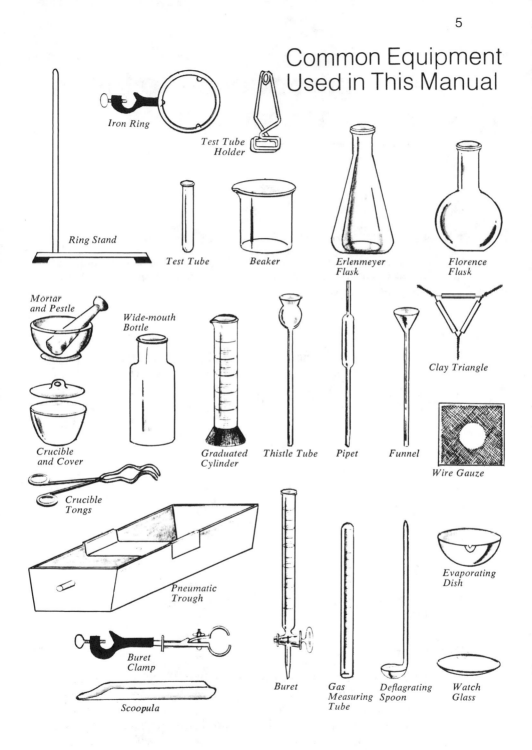

Iron Ring

Test Tube Holder

Ring Stand

Test Tube

Beaker

Erlenmeyer Flask

Florence Flask

Mortar and Pestle

Wide-mouth Bottle

Crucible and Cover

Graduated Cylinder

Thistle Tube

Pipet

Funnel

Clay Triangle

Wire Gauze

Crucible Tongs

Pneumatic Trough

Evaporating Dish

Buret Clamp

Buret

Gas Measuring Tube

Deflagrating Spoon

Watch Glass

Scoopula

1 Introduction to the Laboratory

Purpose

(a) To become acquainted with the facilities of the chemistry laboratory.
(b) To make careful observations of a chemical reaction and to attempt to explain the results.

Introduction

Your teacher will demonstrate the facilities of your chemistry laboratory, including the safety facilities and the locations of the various pieces of apparatus which you will be using. If necessary, your teacher will demonstrate the proper use of the laboratory burner and the graduated cylinder.

Apparatus

10 mL graduated cylinder   iron ring
150 mm test tubes (4)   ring stand
400 mL beaker   burner
wire gauze

Materials

0.25 mol/L hydrochloric acid   mossy zinc
  solution   copper wire

Procedure

A.   Using a graduated cylinder, place 10 mL of 0.25 mol/L hydrochloric acid in a 150 mm test tube. Add 1 piece of mossy zinc. *(1) If there is a reaction, what do you observe, and where is it occurring?* If there is no reaction, warm the test tube briefly (about 20 s) in a hot water bath (Fig. 1-1). *(2) If heating is necessary, what is its effect?*

6

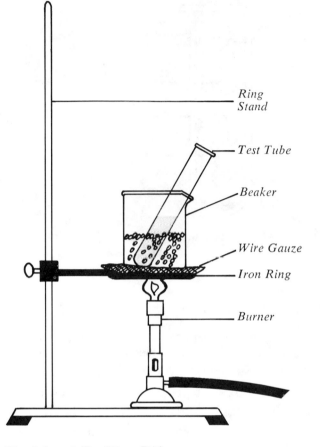

Fig. 1-1   A Hot Water Bath

B.   Using a graduated cylinder, place 10 mL of 0.25 mol/L hydrochloric acid in a second test tube. Add 1 piece of copper wire. *(3) If there is a reaction, what do you observe, and where is it occurring?* If there is no reaction, warm the test tube briefly (about 20 s) in a hot water bath. *(4) If heating is necessary, what is its effect?*

C.   Half-fill a test tube with 0.25 mol/L hydrochloric acid. Wrap one end of a length of copper wire around a piece of zinc metal and place it in the hydrochloric acid, as shown in Fig. 1-2. *(5) If there is a reaction, what do you observe, and where is it occurring?*

D.   Try again, using a new piece of zinc wrapped with a new piece of copper wire. Place the metals in a *dry* test tube. Add the hydrochloric acid slowly down the inner wall of the test tube until something happens. *(6) What do you observe?*

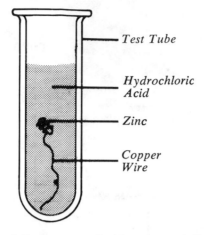

Fig. 1-2 Apparatus for Experiment 1, Part C

Concluding Questions

(1) Based on your observations in parts A and B, what result would you have predicted in part C when the copper-zinc combination was placed in the hydrochloric acid?

(2) How do the results of parts A and B compare with the results of parts C and D?

(3) How do the results of parts C and D compare with each other?

(4) Can you propose a reasonable explanation for the results of this experiment?

2 Household Chemicals

Purpose

To observe some chemical reactions of common household chemicals and to identify two unknown chemicals.

Introduction

In this experiment you will observe the chemical properties of five household chemicals: sugar, baking soda, table salt, Epsom salts, and potassium iodide (added to salt to prevent goiter).

You will observe the behaviour of these chemicals with solutions of silver nitrate and lead nitrate. Finally, you will be asked to identify two of these household chemicals given to you as unknowns.

Apparatus

150 mm test tubes (12)   medicine droppers (2)
10 mL graduated cylinder   test tube holder

Materials

sugar   potassium iodide
baking soda   0.1 mol/L lead nitrate
salt   0.1 mol/L silver nitrate
Epsom salts

Procedure

A.   Prepare a data table as shown. Record all experimental results in the data table as soon as you obtain them.

Data Table 2-1

Chemical	Lead Nitrate	Silver Nitrate
Sugar Baking soda Salt Epsom salts Potassium iodide Unknown 1 Unknown 2		

B. In a test tube place approximately 0.1 g of sugar (measured by comparison with a 0.1 g sample that is on display). Add 5 mL of distilled water to the test tube. Shake the test tube to dissolve the solid. Repeat this procedure using 0.1 g quantities of baking soda, salt, Epsom salts, and potassium iodide in place of the sugar.

C. To each of the five test tubes from part B add 5 drops of lead nitrate and shake. Keep these test tubes for comparison with the results of part E.

D. Using five clean test tubes repeat the procedure of part B. To each of the five test tubes add 5 drops of silver nitrate and shake. CAUTION: Silver nitrate solution causes brown or black stains on skin or clothing. Wash away any spills with plenty of water. Keep these test tubes for comparison with the results of part E.

E. Obtain two unknown household chemicals from your teacher. Use the results of this experiment to identify them.

Concluding Questions

(1) What is the identity of the first unknown?

(2) How do you know?

(3) What is the identity of the second unknown?

(4) How do you know?

3 Observing Chemical Reactions

Purpose

To observe the results when a number of substances are brought together and to decide whether or not a reaction has occurred.

Introduction

In every chemical reaction, one kind of matter is changed into another kind of matter. Sometimes the change is a simple one, as when magnesium metal burns in air to form a white powder. Other chemical changes, such as the digestion of food by our bodies, are the results of thousands of different reactions.

How do we tell when a reaction has occurred? Sometimes chemists can decide this only by using sophisticated machines, but usually something happens during a reaction that we can detect by using our senses (sight, touch, hearing, taste, and smell).

Because so many compounds can be harmful to the body, you should *never* taste an unknown substance. Similarly, the odours of many substances are harmful, and your teacher will demonstrate the correct way to smell a substance.

In this experiment, you will use your senses of sight, smell, and touch to determine whether or not iron(III) chloride, hydrochloric acid, and nitric acid undergo reactions when brought into contact with different substances.

Apparatus

150 mm test tubes (6)
felt-tip pen
spatula

stirring rod
watch glass

Materials

iron(III) chloride
potassium thiocyanate
potassium hexacyanoferrate(II)
distilled water
0.1 mol/L silver nitrate
6 mol/L hydrochloric acid
6 mol/L nitric acid

red litmus paper
blue litmus paper
aluminum
zinc
tin
copper wire

Procedure

A. Prepare data tables as shown. Record all experimental observations in the data table as soon as you obtain them.

Data Table 3-1

Solution	Colour
Iron(III) chloride Potassium thiocyanate Potassium hexacyanoferrate(II) Silver nitrate	

Data Table 3-2

Solution	Observations on Mixing With Iron(III) Chloride
Potassium thiocyanate Potassium hexacyanoferrate(II) Silver nitrate	

Data Table 3-3

Substance	Observations on the Addition of	
	Hydrochloric Acid	Nitric Acid
Red litmus Blue litmus Aluminum Zinc Tin Copper		

EXPERIMENTS WITH IRON(III) CHLORIDE

B. Number each of six 150 mm test tubes from 1 through 6. Using a felt-tip pen or china marker and the inside front cover of this laboratory manual, mark off the volume corresponding to 3 mL on each of the test tubes. To each of test tubes 1, 2, and 3, add an amount of iron(III) chloride crystals no larger than the head of a match. To test tube 4, add a similar amount of potassium thiocyanate crystals. To test tube 5, add a similar amount of potassium hexacyanoferrate(II) crystals. Add distilled water to the 3 mL mark in each of the five test tubes, and shake each test tube gently to dissolve the crystals. To test tube 6, add silver nitrate solution to the 3 mL mark. **CAUTION: Silver nitrate solution causes brown or black stains on skin and clothing. Wash away any spills with plenty of water.**

C. Add the contents of test tube 4 to test tube 1. Add the contents of test tube 5 to test tube 2. Add the contents of test tube 6 to test tube 3. *(1) Did a reaction occur when any of the solutions were mixed? (2) If so, what evidence of your senses supported your answer?* Dispose of the contents of the test tubes. Wash all test tubes thoroughly in preparation for part D.

EXPERIMENTS WITH HYDROCHLORIC ACID

D. Add hydrochloric acid to the 3 mL mark in each of four numbered test tubes. Use a stirring rod to transfer a drop of hydrochloric acid from one of the test tubes to a piece of red litmus paper on a watch glass. In the same way, transfer a drop of hydrochloric acid to a piece of blue litmus paper.

E. To test tube 1 add a small, pea-sized piece of aluminum. To test tube 2 add a small piece of zinc. To test tube 3 add a small piece of tin. To test tube 4 add a small piece of copper wire. *(3) What evidence is there that a reaction occurred in any of the above tests?* Dispose of the liquid contents of each test tube. Discard the solids into the waste container provided. Wash all test tubes thoroughly in preparation for part F.

EXPERIMENTS WITH NITRIC ACID

F. Repeat the steps of parts D and E, using nitric acid instead of hydrochloric acid. **CAUTION: Nitric acid causes yellow stains on skin and burns holes in clothing. Wash away any spills with plenty of water.** *(4) What evidence is there that a reaction occurred in any of the tests?*

Concluding Questions

(1) What reactions do hydrochloric acid and nitric acid have in common?

(2) In what ways do hydrochloric acid and nitric acid differ in their reactions?

(3) Based on your observations during this experiment, what are the types of evidence of reaction that you should expect to find when two substances are brought together?

4 Observing More Chemical Reactions

Purpose

To observe what happens when sodium hydroxide and ammonia are tested with different reagents and to note the similarities and the differences in their chemical behaviour.

Introduction

Sodium hydroxide and ammonia are two common substances that are known as *bases*. Thus, they should show some similarities in their chemical behaviour. However, they are different substances, and so there should be some differences in their behaviour as well.

In this experiment you will test aqueous solutions of sodium hydroxide and ammonia with different substances. Then you will decide the ways in which their chemical behaviour is similar, and the ways in which their behaviour is different.

Apparatus

100 mL beaker
stirring rod
150 mm test tubes (5)
felt-tip marker

Bunsen burner
medicine dropper
test tube holder

Materials

red litmus paper
blue litmus paper
6 mol/L hydrochloric acid
6 mol/L nitric acid

0.1 mol/L silver nitrate
copper(II) sulfate
6 mol/L sodium hydroxide
6 mol/L aqueous ammonia

Procedure

A. Prepare a data table as shown. Record all experimental observations in the data table as soon as you obtain them.

Data Table 4-1

Substance	Observations on the Addition of	
	Sodium hydroxide	Ammonia
Red litmus Blue litmus		
Hydrochloric acid Nitric acid		

Silver nitrate
    (i) + 10 drops base
    (ii) + 3 mL base		

Copper(II) sulfate
    (i) + 10 drops base
    (ii) + 3 mL base
    (iii) + heat		

EXPERIMENTS WITH SODIUM HYDROXIDE

B. Place 25 mL of 6 mol/L sodium hydroxide solution in a beaker.
Use a stirring rod to transfer a drop of the solution to a piece of
red litmus paper on a watch glass. In the same way, transfer a
drop of the solution to a piece of blue litmus paper.

C. Number each of five 150 mm test tubes from 1 through 5. Using a
felt-tip pen or china marker and the inside front cover of this
laboratory manual, mark off the volume corresponding to 3 mL
on each of the test tubes. To test tube 1 add 6 mol/L hydrochloric
acid to the 3 mL mark. To test tube 2 add 3 mL of 6 mol/L nitric
acid. To test tube 3 add 3 mL of 0.1 mol/L silver nitrate solution.
In test tube 4 place 0.1 g of copper(II) sulfate (measured by
comparison with the amount in a test tube taped to the copper(II)
sulfate reagent bottle). Then add 3 mL of water to test tube 4,
heat the test tube over a Bunsen burner flame to dissolve the
crystals, and cool under the cold water tap.

D. Use test tube 5 to add 3 mL of sodium hydroxide solution to test
tube 1. In the same way, add 3 mL of sodium hydroxide solution
to test tube 2. Use a medicine dropper to add 10 drops of sodium

hydroxide solution to test tube 3. Shake well to mix and note what happens. Then use test tube 5 to add an additional 3 mL of sodium hydroxide to test tube 3. Use a medicine dropper to add 10 drops of sodium hydroxide solution to test tube 4. Shake well to mix and note what happens. Then use test tube 5 to add an additional 3 mL of sodium hydroxide to test tube 4. Finally, carefully heat test tube 4 to boiling over a Bunsen burner flame. Dispose of the contents of each test tube. Wash all test tubes thoroughly in preparation for parts E, F, and G.

EXPERIMENTS WITH AMMONIA

E. Repeat part B, using 6 mol/L aqueous ammonia instead of sodium hydroxide.

F. Next, use the numbered test tubes as in part C. Place 3 mL of hydrochloric acid in test tube 1; 3 mL of nitric acid in test tube 2; and 3 mL of silver nitrate solution in test tube 3. In test tube 4 again place 0.1 g of copper(II) sulfate, add 3 mL of water, heat the test tube to dissolve the crystals, and cool under cold water.

G. Use test tube 5 to add 3 mL of ammonia to each of test tubes 1 and 2. Add 10 drops of ammonia to test tube 3. Shake well, and note what happens. Use test tube 5 to add an additional 3 mL of ammonia to test tube 3. Add 10 drops of ammonia to test tube 4. Shake well, and note what happens. Use test tube 5 to add an additional 3 mL of ammonia to test tube 4. Finally, carefully heat test tube 4 to boiling.

Concluding Questions

(1) In what ways do sodium hydroxide and ammonia behave similarly in these chemical reactions?

(2) In what ways do sodium hydroxide and ammonia behave differently in these chemical reactions?

5 Accuracy and Precision

Purpose

To determine the mass per millilitre of water by two different methods and to determine the accuracy and the precision of the results.

Introduction

When we make scientific measurements, we should be concerned with both the accuracy and the precision of the measurements. Accuracy represents the closeness of a measurement to the true or accepted value. Scientists indicate the accuracy of a measurement by calculating the percent error:

$$\text{Percent Error} = \frac{\text{Difference Between Accepted Value and Measured Value}}{\text{Accepted Value}} \times 100$$

Precision is the term used to describe how well a group of measurements made on the same object or event under the same conditions actually agree with one another. The precision of a measurement is indicated by the number of digits in the measurement. That is, we use just enough digits (called significant digits) to indicate the precision of the measurement. The more significant digits that are used for a measurement, the more precise the measurement is. The number of significant digits in a measurement is defined as the number of digits that are known with certainty plus one digit (the last one) which is uncertain. When we state that the mass of an object is 14.6 g, we are indicating that we are certain about the 1 and the 4 but that the last digit might not be a 6. That is, we are certain that the mass of the object is between 14 g and 15 g, but we are not certain how close to 14 g or to 15 g the measurement really is. If we state that the mass of the object is 14.63 g, we are indicating that the mass of the object will always be between 14.6 g and 14.7 g no matter how many times it is measured.

18

In this experiment, we shall determine the mass per millilitre of water by two methods. We shall use the same measurement of the mass of the water in each method. However, the volume of the water will be determined from the dimensions of the beaker in the first method, and by pouring the water into a graduated cylinder in the second method. Each method will be used in triplicate, and the accuracy and the precision of the results obtained from each method will be calculated.

The volume of the beaker is calculated using the formula

$$V = \pi r^2 h$$

where V is the volume of the beaker; r is the radius of the beaker; h is the height of the beaker; and π is a constant whose value to 4 digits is 3.142. The litre is defined as one thousandth of a cubic metre, and the millilitre is one thousandth of a litre.

Apparatus

100 mL beakers (3)   ruler
100 mL graduated cylinder   felt-tip pen

Procedure

A. Prepare a data table as shown. Record all experimental results as soon as you obtain them. Complete the remainder of the data table as soon as you have enough data to do so.

Data Table 5-1

Measurements and Results	#1	#2	#3
Height of beaker (to mark)	_____cm	_____cm	_____cm
Radius of beaker	_____cm	_____cm	_____cm
Calculated volume of beaker	_____mL	_____mL	_____mL
Mass of empty beaker	_____g	_____g	_____g
Mass of beaker and water	_____g	_____g	_____g
Mass of water	_____g	_____g	_____g
Temperature of water	_____°C	_____°C	_____°C
Mass per millilitre of water (first method)	_____g/mL	_____g/mL	_____g/mL
Volume of water measured with graduated cylinder	_____mL	_____mL	_____mL
Mass per millilitre of water (second method)	_____g/mL	_____g/mL	_____g/mL

B. Using a felt-tip pen or china marker, make a mark on a 100 mL beaker about 2 cm from the top. Determine the height of the beaker from the bottom to the mark. Determine the radius of the beaker.

C. Determine the mass of the empty beaker. Carefully fill the beaker to the mark with water. Determine the mass of the beaker and water.

D. Measure the temperature of the water.

E. Pour the water into a 100 mL graduated cylinder. Carefully measure the volume of the water. Water tends to creep up the walls of a container, forming a curved surface called a concave meniscus. The volume of the water should be measured at the bottom of the meniscus. The proper eye level for reading a volume is shown in Fig. 5-1.

F. Repeat parts B through E with a second and a third beaker.

G. Using the data obtained in parts B and F, calculate the volume of each beaker up to the mark. This is also the volume of the water used in parts C and F since each beaker was filled to the mark with water. Use the data obtained in parts C and F to calculate the mass of the water in each beaker. Using these mass and volume

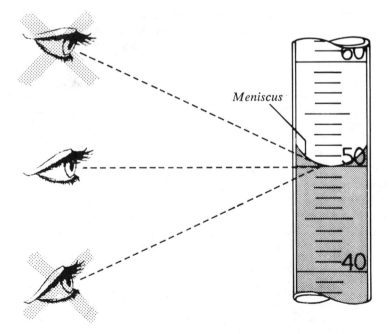

Meniscus

Fig. 5-1   Proper Eye Level for Reading a Graduated Cylinder

data, calculate the mass per millilitre of water for each beaker. This is the first method.

H. Use the mass data obtained in parts C and F and the volume data obtained in parts E and F to calculate the mass per millilitre of water for each beaker. This is the second method.

Concluding Questions

(1) What is the average mass per millilitre of water as determined by using the first method? Use an appropriate number of significant digits to indicate the precision of this average.

(2) Why did you use the number of significant digits that you have in your answer to question 1?

(3) What was the percent error in the mass per millilitre of water as determined by using the first method? Use the answer to question 1 as the measured value. Use the average temperature of the water to obtain the accepted value from Table 5-1.

Table 5-1

Temperature Range (°C)	Mass per Millilitre of Water (g/mL)
0 – 12	1.000
13 – 18	0.999
19 – 23	0.998
24 – 27	0.997
28 – 30	0.996

(4) What are some possible sources of error in the first method?

(5) What is the average mass per millilitre of water as determined by using the second method? Use an appropriate number of significant digits to indicate the precision of this average.

(6) Why did you use the number of significant digits that you have in your answer to question 5?

(7) What was the percent error in the mass per millilitre of water as determined by using the second method? Use the answer to question 5 as the measured value. The accepted value has already been obtained for question 3.

(8) What are some possible sources of error in the second method?

(9) Which method gave the more accurate result?

(10) Which method gave the more precise result?

6 Mass as a Function of Volume

Purpose

To determine the relationship between the mass and the volume of a solid substance.

Introduction

The mass of a solid substance depends on the size of the sample. The mass of any object is a function of its size. The volume of a solid substance is also a function of the size of the sample. If the solid has a regular shape, its volume can be calculated from its dimensions (e.g., length, width, and thickness, or diameter and height). However, many solids are irregular in shape. The volumes of irregular solids can be measured by the method of water displacement. In this method, the solid is submerged in a known volume of water. As the solid sinks, it displaces a volume of water equal to its own volume. The new volume equals the combined volumes of the water and the solid. The change in volume equals the volume of the irregular solid.

Intuitively, we might expect a relationship between the mass and the volume of a solid. Since they are both functions of the size of the solid, they are likely to be related to one another. That is, changing the volume of a solid causes a change in the mass of the solid. We might expect that doubling the volume of a solid would double its mass or halving its volume would halve its mass. If this were to be a correct guess, we could say that the mass and the volume of a solid are directly proportional to one another.

We will determine by a graphical method whether the masses and volumes of various quantities of the same solid substance are directly proportional. The mass of each sample will be plotted on the vertical axis, and the corresponding volume of each sample will be plotted on the horizontal axis. If the mass and the volume of a solid are directly proportional, the points of the graph will fall along a straight line which passes through the origin (the point at which the mass and volume both equal zero).

The equation which represents a direct proportionality is $y = kx$, where y is the variable plotted along the vertical axis (mass), x is the variable plotted along the horizontal axis (volume), and k is the constant of proportionality. The value of k is easily calculated by solving the equation

$$k = \frac{y}{x} = \frac{\text{mass}}{\text{volume}}$$

Substitution of any one pair of the values of mass and volume will allow us to solve the equation for k. If the mass and volume of a solid are directly proportional, *any other* pair of values will give the same value for k.

Apparatus

50 mL graduated cylinder

Materials

different-sized samples of the same solid substance

Procedure

A. Prepare a data table as shown. Record all experimental results as soon as you obtain them. Complete the remainder of the data table as soon as you have enough data to do so.

Data Table 6-1

Measurements and Results	#1	#2	#3	#4	#5
Mass of sample	——g	——g	——g	——g	——g
Volume of water	——mL	——mL	——mL	——mL	——mL
Volume of water and sample	——mL	——mL	——mL	——mL	——mL
Volume of sample	——mL	——mL	——mL	——mL	——mL
$k = \dfrac{\text{mass}}{\text{volume}}$	——g/mL	——g/mL	——g/mL	——g/mL	——g/mL

B. Obtain several samples of the same solid substance as directed by your teacher.

C. Determine the mass of one of the samples. Place 25 mL of water in a 50 mL graduated cylinder. Read and record the volume of the water to the nearest 0.1 mL. Tilt the graduated cylinder and allow the sample to slide gently down the inside wall. The sample must be completely submerged in the water. Tap the graduated cylinder gently to force any air bubbles trapped by the sample to the surface. Read and record the volume of the water plus the sample to the nearest 0.1 mL. Empty the graduated cylinder by pouring the water down the sink and placing the solid in the container provided by your teacher.

D. Repeat part C for the remaining samples.

E. Using your data, plot a graph of the mass of each sample (vertical axis) against its volume (horizontal axis).

Concluding Questions

(1) Does your graph show that the mass and the volume of a solid are directly proportional?

(2) Why would you expect the graph to pass through the origin whether the relationship between the mass and the volume of a solid is a direct proportionality or not?

(3) What can you say about the constancy of the mass/volume ratios?

(4) Density is defined as the mass of an object per unit volume of the object, and the derived SI unit for density is kilograms per cubic metre (kg/m^3). What is the density of your solid substance? (One litre is one thousandth of one cubic metre.)

(5) Based on your calculations, what is the mass of the largest sample that could have been used in this experiment?

(6) Why must air bubbles trapped by the sample be forced to the surface of the water in the graduated cylinder?

7 Melting Points of Solids

Purpose

To determine the melting point of a pure, unknown solid and to determine the effect of an impurity on the melting point of a compound.

Introduction

Strictly speaking, the melting point of a pure solid is the temperature at which the solid and the molten liquid can exist together. The melting point is a physical property characteristic of the substance and can be used to identify the substance. In practice, chemists usually do not measure this temperature. Instead, they heat the solid slowly and continuously until it is completely melted. The temperatures between which the first crystal begins to melt and the last crystal disappears define the melting point range of the substance. The slower the rate of heating, the more nearly the melting point range reflects the true melting point of the compound. Pure substances usually have melting point ranges of 1 °C or less.

In this experiment you will determine the melting point of a pure compound. In addition, you will determine the effect of an impurity on the melting point of a compound.

Apparatus

watch glass
150 mm test tube
melting point tubes
ruler
rubber band
thermometer
250 mL beaker
one-hole rubber stopper for
    thermometer

buret clamp
iron ring
wire gauze
ring stand
burner
wire loop stirrer
stirring rod
file

Materials

pure, unknown compound
camphor

Procedure

A. Place a small quantity of sample on a clean watch glass and pulverize the sample by rubbing it with the bottom of a clean test tube. Do not rub so hard that you break the test tube or the watch glass. Carefully force a portion of the sample into a melting point tube by pushing the open end of the tube into the powdered sample. Invert the tube and lightly draw a file several times across the tube to shake the sample into the closed end. Repeat this process until the tube contains sample to a depth of 5 mm. Do not add too much sample to the tube at any one time.

B. Place a small quantity of sample and an equal volume of camphor on a watch glass. Mix them thoroughly with a stirring rod. Pulverize the mixture by rubbing it with the bottom of a clean test tube. Place this mixture to a depth of 5 mm in a second melting point tube.

C. Place a small rubber band about 5 cm above the thermometer bulb. Insert the melting point tubes under the rubber band, one on either side of the thermometer (Fig. 7-1). Note which tube contains the pure unknown compound and which contains the mixture. The positions of the tubes should be adjusted so that the samples are located next to the thermometer bulb. Support the thermometer in a 250 mL beaker about two-thirds full of water. The open ends of the melting point tubes must be above the water level.

D. Heat the water very slowly and with constant stirring. Try to obtain a rate of temperature increase of not more than $3°C/min$. ($1°C/20$ s). Watch the solids in the melting point tubes carefully. *For each solid,* note the temperature at which the first crystal begins to melt and the temperature at which the last crystal disappears. Check the melting point of your unknown with your teacher. If your melting point range is too wide or if your values differ from the accepted value by more than one or two degrees, you will have to make a new determination. Repeat until you obtain acceptable values. Use a new melting point tube for each trial. Finally, obtain from your teacher a list of possible unknowns and their melting points.

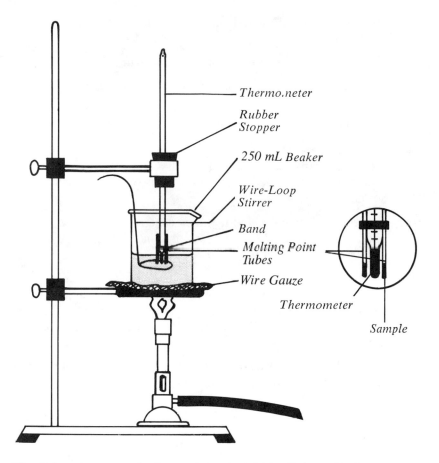

Fig. 7-1   Apparatus for Determining the Melting Points of Solids

Concluding Questions

(1) In which melting point tube did the crystals begin to melt first?

(2) At what temperature did the crystals of the pure compound begin to melt?

(3) At what temperature did the last crystal of the pure compound just disappear?

(4) What is the melting point range of the pure compound?

(5) At what temperature did the crystals of the mixture begin to melt?

(6) At what temperature did the last crystal of the mixture just disappear?

(7) What is the melting point range of the mixture?

(8) What is the identity of your pure unknown compound?

(9) What is the effect of an impurity on the melting point of a compound?

(10) If you had forgotten which melting point tube contained the pure unknown compound and which contained the mixture, could you have distinguished them on the basis of this experiment? If so, how?

(11) Students occasionally find that they can get a 3°C/min temperature rise, but as they near the melting point their tension increases and the temperature rises at a rate of 5 or 6°C/min. What effect, if any, would this have on the melting point range?

(12) You are given two colourless solids, each having a melting point range of 80-82°C. Describe a simple procedure by which you would determine whether the two solids are identical or different.

(13) What effect does the addition of salt have on the melting point of ice? What practical use is made of this effect?

8 The Cooling Curve of a Pure Substance and of a Mixture

Purpose

To determine the freezing point of a pure substance from its cooling curve and to determine the effect of an impurity on the cooling curve of the pure substance.

Introduction

If a pure substance is heated slowly, it melts at a characteristic temperature. For example, the melting point of ice is 0°C. In the same way, if the liquid is cooled slowly, it solidifies at a constant temperature. The freezing point of water is also 0°C. As long as solid and liquid exist together, the temperature will remain constant.

A typical cooling curve for a pure substance is shown in Fig. 8-1. The freezing point (or melting point) is easily determined by reading on the vertical axis the temperature corresponding to point A on the diagram.

Sometimes a pure substance does not begin to solidify until the temperature is several degrees below its freezing point. A substance which remains in the liquid state at a temperature below its normal freezing point is said to be *supercooled*. Once the substance starts to freeze and the first crystals appear, the temperature rises quickly until it reaches the normal freezing point, then stays constant until the substance is completely solid. If supercooling occurs, there will be a dip in the cooling curve as shown in Fig. 8-1.

In this experiment you will construct the cooling curve for a pure substance (acetamide) and determine the freezing point of the substance. Then you will add an impurity (camphor) to the pure substance, construct a cooling curve for the impure mixture, and note the effect of the impurity on the freezing point of the pure substance.

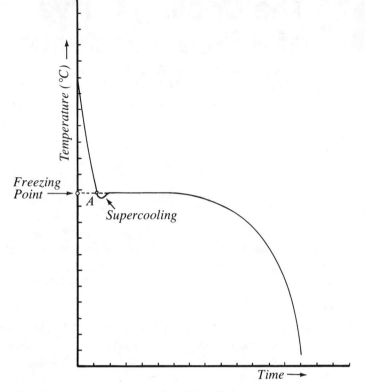

Fig. 8-1   Cooling Curve for a Pure Substance

Apparatus

400 mL beaker   burner
wire gauze   test tubes (2)
ring stand   thermometer
iron ring   buret clamp

Materials

acetamide   camphor

Procedure

A.   Prepare a data table as shown. Record all observations in the data table as soon as you obtain them.

Data Table 8-1

Temperature of Unknown at Half-Minute Intervals		Temperature of Mixture at Half-Minute Intervals	
Time (min)	Temperature (°C)	Time (min)	Temperature (°C)
0.0		0.0	
0.5		0.5	
1.0		1.0	
1.5		1.5	
2.0		2.0	
2.5		2.5	
3.0		3.0	
3.5		3.5	
4.0		4.0	
4.5		4.5	
5.0		5.0	
5.5		5.5	
6.0		6.0	
6.5		6.5	
7.0		7.0	
7.5		7.5	
8.0		8.0	
8.5		8.5	
9.0		9.0	
9.5		9.5	
10.0		10.0	
10.5		10.5	
11.0		11.0	
11.5		11.5	
12.0		12.0	
12.5		12.5	
13.0		13.0	
13.5		13.5	
14.0		14.0	
14.5		14.5	

B. Fill a 400 mL beaker two-thirds full of water. Place it on a wire gauze on a ring stand and begin heating it with a small flame. Meanwhile, fill a 150 mm test tube about one-fourth full of crystals of pure acetamide. Clamp the test tube in the water bath, and heat the water almost to the boiling point. When the compound has melted, insert a thermometer. When the temperature reaches about 95°C, remove the test tube from the water bath and swing it to the side, allowing it to remain clamped to the ring stand. Record the initial temperature. Stirring *gently,* record the temperature to the nearest 0.1°C every half-minute. Then stop stirring, but record the temperature at half-minute intervals until it has dropped to about 65°C. *(1) At what temperature do the first crystals appear? (2) At what temperature does the substance become completely solid?*

C. To a clean test tube add camphor until the test tube is about one-eighth full. Transfer the camphor to the test tube containing the solidified acetamide. Place the test tube in the water bath and heat while stirring until the mixture is completely melted and its temperature is about 95°C. Then remove from the heat and record the temperature at half-minute intervals as in part B. *(3) At what temperature do the first crystals appear? (4) At what temperature does the mixture become completely solid?*

D. Remelt the mixture and discard it in the container provided by your teacher.

E. Construct a cooling curve for the pure compound by plotting temperature (vertical axis) against time (horizontal axis). Locate point A on your cooling curve. In the same way, construct a cooling curve for the mixture.

Concluding Questions

(1) Does the pure substance show any indication of supercooling when it freezes? If so, what is the evidence?

(2) What is the melting point of the pure substance?

(3) How does the cooling curve for the impure substance differ from that of the pure substance?

(4) What is the effect of an impurity on the freezing point of a pure substance?

(5) What effect would the addition of an organic compound such as ethylene glycol have on the freezing point of water? What practical use is made of this effect?

9 Physical and Chemical Properties

Purpose

To observe and identify physical and chemical properties.

Introduction

Physical properties are properties which can be determined without changing the composition of a substance. Chemical properties are those properties which can be determined when a change in the composition of a substance occurs.

Physical changes involve changes in physical properties such as shape or state, with no new substances being formed. Chemical changes involve changes in composition and therefore the formation of new substances.

In this experiment you will examine the physical and chemical properties of a number of substances.

Apparatus

150 mm test tubes (8)   10 mL graduated cylinder
burner   150 mL beakers (2)
iron ring   watch glass
wire gauze   spatula
ring stand   medicine dropper

Materials

copper(II) sulfate pentahydrate   lead nitrate
copper(II) nitrate   0.5 mol/L sodium thiosulfate
zinc oxide   potassium iodide
iodine   potassium chloride
trichlorotrifluoroethane (TTE)   2 mol/L hydrochloric acid

Procedure

A. Prepare a data table as shown. Record all experimental results in the data table as soon as you obtain them.

Data Table 9-1

Part	Observations	Type of Property
B		
C		
D		
E		
F		
G		
H		
I		

B. Place about 0.25 g (measured by comparison with a sample on display) of blue copper(II) sulfate crystals in a test tube and heat until no further change is observed. Cool and add 5 drops of water.

C. Place 3 or 4 crystals of copper(II) nitrate in a clean dry test tube and heat until the crystals begin to glow.

D. Place about 0.25 g (measured by comparison with a sample on display) of zinc oxide in a test tube and heat until you observe a change. Allow it to cool for 1 min and observe.

E. Add 1 crystal of iodine to 1 mL of TTE in a test tube and shake.

F. Place 1 crystal of iodine in a dry 150 mL beaker. Place a watch glass over this beaker and add cold water to the watch glass. Heat the beaker supported by a wire gauze on an iron ring until the iodine crystal disappears. Allow to cool and then scrape off any material on the bottom of the watch glass or side of the beaker. Add this material to 1 mL of TTE in a test tube. If you have difficulty scraping off enough, add a drop of TTE directly to the material.

G. Add 5 mL of 0.5 mol/L sodium thiosulfate to a test tube containing 5 mL of 2 mol/L hydrochloric acid.

H. Add a few crystals of lead nitrate to 5 mL of water. Dissolve a few crystals of potassium iodide in 5 mL of water in another test tube. Mix the two solutions.

I. Dissolve 0.1 g of potassium chloride in 5 mL of water in a 150 mL beaker. Place a watch glass over the beaker and heat until all the water has disappeared.

Concluding Questions

(1) What types of evidence helped you decide whether you were observing a physical or a chemical property?

(2) What types of evidence helped you decide whether you were observing a physical or a chemical change?

(3) Does a change in colour always indicate that a chemical reaction has taken place? Support your answer by referring to this experiment.

(4) What types of physical properties did you observe in this experiment?

(5) What types of chemical properties did you observe in this experiment?

10 The Physical Properties of a Compound

Purpose

To determine the physical properties of a compound.

Introduction

Physical properties are properties which can be determined without changing the composition of a substance. In this experiment, we will determine the state, colour, odour, solubility in water, volatility (ease of evaporation), density, and boiling point of trichlorotrifluoroethane (TTE).

Density is the mass of a substance per unit volume of the substance. The SI unit for density is kilograms per cubic metre (kg/m^3). In this experiment, the mass in grams of one millilitre of TTE will be determined, and this quantity will have to be converted to the mass in kilograms of one cubic metre of TTE. The factor-label method can be used to carry out this conversion if we recall that the litre is defined as one thousandth of a cubic metre. For example, if one millilitre of a substance has a mass of one gram, its density is 1000 kg/m^3:

$$x \text{ kg/m}^3 = \frac{1\,\cancel{g}}{1\,\cancel{mL}} \times \frac{1 \text{ kg}}{1000\,\cancel{g}} \times \frac{1000\,\cancel{mL}}{1\,\cancel{L}} \times \frac{1000\,\cancel{L}}{1 \text{ m}^3} = 1000 \text{ kg/m}^3$$

Apparatus

10 mL graduated cylinder	filter paper
150 mm test tubes (3)	wire gauze
200 mm test tube	burner
medicine dropper	thermometer

boiling chips
600 mL beaker
iron ring
ring stand

buret clamp
two-hole rubber stopper
(to fit 200 mm test tube)

Materials

trichlorotrifluoroethane (TTE)

Procedure

A.   Prepare a data table as shown. Record all experimental results in the data table as soon as you obtain them. Complete the remainder of the table as soon as you have enough data to do so.

Data Table 10-1

State of TTE	
Colour of TTE	
Odour of TTE	
Solubility of TTE in water	
Volatility of TTE (compared to water)	
Mass of empty graduated cylinder	_____ g
Mass of graduated cylinder and TTE	_____ g
Mass of 5.0 mL of TTE	_____ g
Mass of 1.0 mL of TTE	_____ g
Density of TTE	_____ kg/m³
Boiling point of TTE	_____ °C

B.   Place 1 mL of TTE in a test tube. Observe the state, colour, and odour of the TTE. Use this TTE in part C.

C.   Add 1 mL of distilled water to the test tube containing the 1 mL of TTE. Shake the test tube. *(1) What do you observe?*

D.   Place a few drops of TTE on a piece of filter paper and blow on the spot of TTE. Repeat, using a few drops of water. *(2) How does the volatility of the TTE compare with the volatility of water?*

E.   Determine the mass of a dry 10 mL graduated cylinder to the nearest 0.01 g. Add 5 mL of TTE to this graduated cylinder, using a medicine dropper to adjust the bottom of the meniscus to the 5.0 mL mark. Determine the mass of the graduated cylinder containing the 5.0 mL of TTE. Use this 5.0 mL of TTE in part F.

F.   In a 200 mm test tube, place 5 mL of TTE. Add a small boiling chip to the liquid to promote smooth boiling. Place a two-hole rubber stopper fitted with a thermometer in the test tube, as shown in Fig. 10-1. The thermometer should be adjusted so that the bulb is about 1 cm above the surface of the liquid. Clamp the test tube to a ring stand. Support a 600 mL beaker, half-filled with water, on a wire gauze placed on an iron ring. Immerse the test tube in the water. The test tube should not touch the bottom of the beaker. Heat the water in the beaker *gently* and watch for changes inside

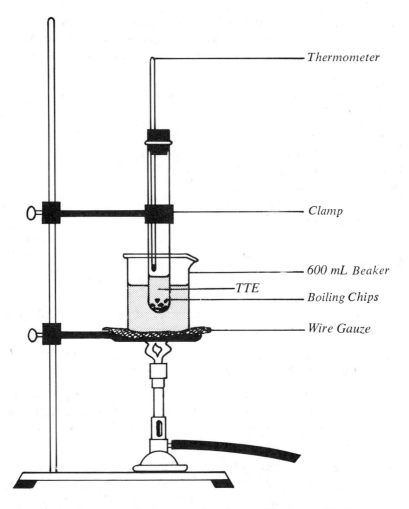

Fig. 10-1   Apparatus for Determining the Boiling Point of TTE

the test tube. Eventually the TTE will boil, and the temperature will remain constant. At that point, droplets of liquid should be condensing on the thermometer and falling back into the liquid in the test tube. The temperature at which the liquid boils is called the boiling point. *(3) If you had heated the water bath faster than suggested, what effect (if any) would this have had on the determination of the boiling point?*

11 Mixtures

Purpose

To prepare a mixture, compare its properties with those of its components, and to determine the percentage by mass of the mixture by separating it into its components.

Introduction

In this experiment you will study some properties of silicon dioxide and sodium chloride. Then you will mix the two substances and compare the properties of the mixture with those of its components. Finally, you will separate the components of the mixture and determine the percentage by mass of silicon dioxide and sodium chloride in the mixture.

Apparatus

150 mm test tubes (3)	wire gauze
10 mL graduated cylinder	burner
stirring rod	watch glass
iron ring	100 mL beaker
ring stand	

Materials

silicon dioxide (granular)   sodium chloride

Procedure

A.   In a test tube place a 0.1 g sample of sodium chloride (measured by comparison with a 0.1 g sample that is on display). *(1) What is the colour of the sodium chloride? (2) What is the appearance of the sodium chloride?* In a second test tube place a 0.1 g sample of silicon dioxide (measured by comparison). *(3) What is the colour of the silicon dioxide? (4) What is the appearance of the silicon dioxide?*

B. Add 3 mL of water to the test tube of sodium chloride and shake it vigorously. *(5) Is sodium chloride soluble in water?* Now add 3 mL of water to the test tube containing silicon dioxide and shake it vigorously. *(6) Is silicon dioxide soluble in water?*

C. Prepare a mixture of sodium chloride and silicon dioxide by mixing (shaking) together 0.2 g of each in a test tube. *(7) How does the colour of the mixture compare with that of the two separate components? (8) How does the appearance of the mixture compare with that of the two separate components?* Add 6 mL of water to the mixture and shake vigorously. *(9) What do you observe? (10) How do you explain this observation?*

D. Prepare a data table as shown. Record all experimental results in the data table as soon as you obtain them. Complete the remainder of the data table as soon as you have enough data to do so.

Data Table 11-1

Mass of empty 100 mL beaker plus watch glass	———————— g
Mass of 100 mL beaker plus watch glass and mixture	———————— g
Mass of mixture	———————— g
Mass of 100 mL beaker plus watch glass and solid after heating	———————— g
Mass of silicon dioxide	———————— g
Mass of sodium chloride	———————— g
Percentage of silicon dioxide in mixture	———————— %
Percentage of sodium chloride in mixture	———————— %

E. Determine the total mass of a clean, dry beaker and watch glass cover to the nearest 0.01 g. Add the mixture obtained from your teacher to this beaker and determine the total mass of the beaker, watch glass, and mixture.

F. Add 20 mL of water to the mixture and stir. *Carefully* decant (pour off) the water without removing any solid. Discard the liquid. Wash the solid by adding 10 mL of water to the beaker, stirring, and decanting the water. Discard the wash water. Repeat the washing with a second 10 mL portion of water. After you have poured off as much water as possible without losing any solid, place the watch glass cover over the beaker with the concave side up.

G.   Heat the beaker until no water can be seen in the beaker or on the watch glass. Allow the apparatus to cool.

H.   Determine the total mass of the beaker, watch glass, and solid residue.

Concluding Questions

(1)   What substance was in the water that was decanted in part F? How do you know?

(2)   What solid substance was left in the beaker? How do you know?

(3)   What difference in physical property did you use to separate the components of the mixture?

(4)   How do the properties of a mixture compare with the properties of its components?

(5)   Based on the percentages calculated by the students in your class, what can you conclude about the percentage composition of a mixture?

12 Percentage Composition

Purpose

To determine the percentage of copper in an oxide of copper.

Introduction

In the early days of chemistry a great controversy arose between two French chemists. J. L. Proust maintained that a compound always had the same percentage composition no matter how it was prepared. His compatriot, C. M. Berthollet, however, argued that a compound should have an infinite number of compositions, depending on the proportions of its components that were used during its preparation. In this experiment, you will determine the percentage of copper in a compound by a method that Proust or Berthollet might have used.

You will mix a known mass of an oxide of copper with a known mass of carbon in a crucible. You will then heat the mixture to the highest temperature possible with your laboratory burner. The quantities have been chosen so that there is sufficient carbon to combine with all of the oxygen in the oxide of copper, forming carbon dioxide gas. Copper metal remains in the crucible, and its mass can be determined. (Your teacher may wish you to perform this experiment twice for the sake of comparing results.)

Apparatus

crucible and cover (1 or 2)   burner
clay triangle   crucible tongs
iron ring   wire gauze
ring stand   spatula

Materials

oxide of copper   Norit A® decolourizing carbon

43

Procedure

A. Prepare a data table as shown. Record all experimental results in the data table as soon as you obtain them. Complete the remainder of the table as soon as you have enough data to do so.

Data Table 12-1

Measurements and Results	#1	#2
Mass of crucible	_____ g	_____ g
Mass of crucible and oxide of copper	_____ g	_____ g
Mass of crucible, oxide of copper, and carbon	_____ g	_____ g
Mass of crucible and copper	_____ g	_____ g
Mass of oxide of copper	_____ g	_____ g
Mass of copper	_____ g	_____ g
Percentage of copper in oxide of copper	_____ %	_____ %

B. Determine the mass of your dry crucible (without the cover) to the nearest 0.01 g.

C. Measure 1.70 g of the oxide of copper on a piece of filter paper, and transfer all of the solid to the crucible. Determine the mass of the crucible and oxide of copper, and subtract from this the mass of the empty crucible to obtain the mass of the oxide of copper in the crucible. *(1) Why is the mass of the oxide of copper on the filter paper not necessarily the same as the mass of the oxide of copper in the crucible?*

D. Measure 0.15 g of Norit A® decolourizing carbon on a piece of filter paper, and transfer all of the carbon to the crucible. Using a spatula, mix the contents of the crucible well. Determine the mass of the crucible containing the oxide of copper and carbon. This mass is not used in any calculations. It is measured merely to ensure that there is 0.15 g of carbon in the crucible.

E. Attach an iron ring to a ring stand. Place the cover on the crucible, and support the covered crucible in a clay triangle on the ring.

F. Heat the mixture in the crucible as strongly as possible for six minutes with your laboratory burner.

G. If you have been told to make a second determination of the percentage of copper, repeat parts B, C, and D using a second crucible, while the first crucible is being heated.

H. Remove the first crucible from the ring stand, and place it on a wire gauze with the cover on. While the first crucible is cooling, place the second, covered crucible in the clay triangle and repeat part F.

I. After allowing the first crucible to cool for at least eight minutes with the cover on, remove the cover and determine the mass of the crucible and contents.

J. Repeat part I with the second crucible.

Concluding Questions

(1) What was the evidence of reaction during the heating process?

(2) Why do you suppose that a large excess of carbon has been avoided in favour of a slight excess?

(3) What was the appearance of the contents of the crucible after heating?

(4) If you had obtained a percentage of copper which was much too large, what should you have expected the appearance of the contents of the crucible to be after heating?

(5) If you were a chemist working during the time of Proust and Berthollet, how could you have used this method of determining the percentage of copper in an oxide of copper to carry out experiments which might help to resolve the controversy?

13 Designing a Model

Purpose

To devise a model to represent an object in a sealed box which can never be opened.

Introduction

Often people involved in science are forced to try to visualize objects which they do not expect to see. The atom is a good example. Scientists have reason to believe that they will never actually see the inside of an atom. However, they have been able to construct a model of the structure of the atom based on experimental evidence.

Bohr developed a solar system model of the atom, but further experimentation led to the development of the quantum mechanical model of the atom which we use today.

We can place ourselves in the same kind of situation in which scientists find themselves with respect to the atom. Consider an object of unknown size, shape, density, and composition sealed in a box. The box can never be opened, and we will never be able to see the object. However, we can perform operations on the box which will help us to learn more and more about the object. Finally, we should be able to develop a mental picture or model of the object.

Apparatus

box containing an object

Procedure

A. Obtain a sealed box containing an unknown object. Perform a series of manipulations on the box and observe the results of each manipulation. You may do anything to the box as long as you do not open or damage it. For example, you can shake it, tilt it, and determine the total mass of the box and the object. (An empty box of the same size will be provided so that you can determine the mass of the box alone.) *(1) What manipulations did you perform, and what information did these yield?*

B. Try to develop a mental picture of the object inside the box. *(2) What is your model of the object?* Test your model and try to improve it by doing further manipulations. *(3) What manipulations did you perform to test and improve your model, and what information did these yield? (4) Did the results from these further manipulations force you to modify your model?*

Concluding Questions

(1) Why must the box not be opened?

(2) What were your most useful manipulations and what made them so useful?

(3) What were your least useful manipulations and why were they not as useful as you had hoped?

(4) What other manipulations would you have liked to perform for which you did not have the necessary equipment?

(5) What information had you hoped to get from the manipulations you were not able to make?

(6) What is the most detailed description of the object in the box that you can write?

14 Line Spectra

Purpose

To observe the line spectra of some elements and to identify several elements by their line spectra.

Introduction

In this experiment, you will observe a continuous spectrum. You will also observe line spectra and compare them to the continuous spectrum. Finally, you will identify some elements by observing their line spectra.

In order to view the spectra you will look through a diffraction grating. The action of a diffraction grating is similar to that of a prism: light is separated into its component colours to produce a spectrum.

Apparatus

gas discharge tubes
incandescent light bulb

diffraction grating
power source

Procedure

A. Your teacher will provide an incandescent light source. Look through the diffraction grating. Draw and label the spectrum you observe. *(1) Is this a continuous or a line spectrum? (2) How do you know?*

B. Using your diffraction grating, observe the spectra produced by several gas discharge tubes. Sketch each spectrum, and be sure to indicate the colour of each observed line.

C. Repeat part B using unknowns provided by your teacher. *(3) What is the identity of each unknown?*

Concluding Questions

(1) How were you able to use the spectrum of each unknown to establish its identity?

(2) Why did each gas show a colour only when electricity was passed through the discharge tube?

(3) What is the difference between a continuous spectrum and a line spectrum?

(4) What do the different colours in a line spectrum represent?

(5) Why do different substances show different spectra?

(6) How are astronomers able to identify chemicals in distant space?

(7) What type of spectrum is produced by hydrogen?

(8) How does the Bohr model of the hydrogen atom explain the spectrum of hydrogen?

(9) What is a practical application of passing electricity through a gas?

15 Flame Colours and Electronic Energy Levels

Purpose

To observe the colours produced when solutions of metal ions are heated to high temperatures, to explain the results in terms of the energy levels of the metal ions, and to use the colours to identify an unknown.

Introduction

When an atom, a molecule, or an ion is heated to a high temperature in a burner flame, one (or more) of its electrons gains energy and is raised to a higher energy level. Later, the electron returns to a lower energy level and gives off its excess energy in the form of light of a characteristic colour. Since there are many atoms in any sample of a substance, all possible jumps from one energy level to another can occur at the same time, each giving off its characteristic colour. The colour that we see is a mixture of all these colours, but the predominant colour is that which corresponds to the most frequently occurring transition.

Apparatus

nichrome test wire	cobalt glass squares (2)
test tubes (10)	burner

Materials

6 mol/L hydrochloric acid	0.5 mol/L strontium nitrate
0.5 mol/L sodium nitrate	0.5 mol/L lithium nitrate
0.5 mol/L sodium chloride	0.5 mol/L potassium nitrate
0.5 mol/L barium nitrate	0.5 mol/L copper(II) nitrate
0.5 mol/L calcium nitrate	sodium chloride

Procedure

A. Prepare a data table as shown. Record all experimental results in the data table as soon as you obtain them.

Data Table 15-1

Substance	Flame Colour
Sodium nitrate solution	
Sodium chloride solution	
Solid sodium chloride	
Barium nitrate solution	
Calcium nitrate solution	
Strontium nitrate solution	
Lithium nitrate solution	
Potassium nitrate solution	
Copper(II) nitrate solution	
Sodium nitrate solution with cobalt glass	
Potassium nitrate solution with cobalt glass	
Sodium nitrate and potassium nitrate solutions with cobalt glass	
Unknown solution	

B. Light the burner and adjust it so that the flame is almost colourless. Hold a nichrome test wire momentarily in the flame. *(1) What do you observe?* CAUTION: Do not heat the glass rod into which the nichrome wire is sealed. The glass may break or melt if it is heated.

C. Wet the nichrome wire in a half-filled test tube of hydrochloric acid, and then place the wire in the colourless flame of your burner. Repeat the process until the wire no longer imparts a colour to the flame. (The wire will, of course, become red hot, but the flame should not be coloured).

D. Using the chart on the inside front cover of this manual as a guide, pour about 3 mL of sodium nitrate solution into a test tube. Dip the tip of the nichrome wire into the solution, and then hold the wire in the flame.

E. Using the procedure of part C, clean the wire. Pour about 3 mL of sodium chloride solution into another test tube. Dip the clean wire into the sodium chloride solution, and hold the wire in the flame.

F. Clean the wire again. Dip the hot wire into a little solid sodium chloride contained in a test tube, and hold the wire in the flame.

G. Using the procedures of parts C and D, test 3 mL samples of solutions of nitrates of barium, calcium, strontium, lithium, potassium, and copper. Clean the wire carefully after each test.

H. Again clean the wire, and retest your 3 mL sample of sodium nitrate solution, but this time observe the result through two thicknesses of cobalt glass. Test the potassium nitrate solution in the same manner.

I. Now mix the solutions of sodium nitrate and potassium nitrate. Clean the nichrome wire, dip it into the mixture, and hold the wire in the flame. Repeat, this time observing the result through two thicknesses of cobalt glass.

J. Obtain an unknown solution from your teacher, and test it in the flame. Observe it also using two thicknesses of cobalt glass.

Concluding Questions

(1) What is the purpose of the procedure you followed in part B?

(2) Is there any difference in the results you obtained in parts D, E, and F?

(3) Is there any difference in the results for strontium and lithium? If so, what is the difference?

(4) Is there any difference in the results for barium and copper? If so, what is the difference?

(5) Is there any difference between the results obtained when the colour produced by the sodium nitrate is viewed directly and when it is viewed through cobalt glass? If so, what is the difference?

(6) Is there any difference between the results obtained when the colour produced by a mixture of sodium nitrate and potassium nitrate is viewed directly and when it is viewed through cobalt glass? If so, what is the difference?

(7) What is the purpose of the cobalt glass?

(8) What is the identity of your unknown?

(9) The energies of light quanta increase gradually as the colour of light changes in this sequence: red → orange → yellow → green → blue → indigo → violet. That is, a quantum of violet light contains much more energy than does a quantum of red light. Which metal has electronic transitions involving the largest energy change?

(10) Which metal has electronic transitions involving the smallest energy change?

(11) What is the order of the metals used in this experiment, when they are arranged according to the *increasing* energies of their electronic transitions?

(12) What do you think is the source of the colours observed in exploding fireworks and during the burning of many kinds of artificial logs?

16 Properties of Metals and Nonmetals

Purpose

To study the properties of a typical metal and a typical nonmetal.

Introduction

Most of the chemical elements can be classed as either metals or nonmetals. Although metals do not all have identical properties, some properties are common to most metals. Similarly, some properties are common to most nonmetals. In this experiment, you will determine some of the properties of metals by studying a typical metal − zinc. You will determine some of the properties of nonmetals by studying a typical nonmetal − sulfur.

Apparatus

crucible cover	iron ring
clay triangle	ring stand
conductivity apparatus	10 mL graduated cylinder
150 mm test tubes (2)	burner

Materials

mossy zinc	1 mol/L hydrochloric acid
zinc strips	steel wool
roll sulfur	

Procedure

A. **Teacher demonstration:** Touch the electrodes of a conductivity apparatus to a strip of zinc and then to a piece of sulfur. *(1) What do you observe in each case?*

B. Attempt to polish a strip of zinc and a piece of sulfur with some steel wool. *(2) What do you observe about the lustre of each?*

C. Attempt to bend a strip of zinc. Attempt to bend a piece of sulfur. *(3) What do you observe about the flexibility of each?*

D. Place a piece of sulfur about the size of a match head and a small piece of mossy zinc well apart on an inverted crucible cover. Place an iron ring on a ring stand so that it is about 25 cm above the top of a burner. Using a clay triangle, support the crucible cover on the ring and heat the cover gently for 2 min. *(4) What do you observe? (5) What can you say about the relative melting points of the two substances?*

E. Place a piece of sulfur the size of a match head into a test tube containing 3 mL of hydrochloric acid. Place a small piece of mossy zinc into a second test tube containing 3 mL of hydrochloric acid. *(6) What do you observe in each case?*

F. Determine the mass of 8 small pieces of mossy zinc. *(7) What is the mass of the zinc?* Drop them into a 10 mL graduated cylinder containing 7 mL of water. *(8) What is the volume occupied by the zinc? (9) What is the mass of 1 cm^3 (i.e., 1 mL) of zinc?*

G. Repeat part F using 4 pieces of roll sulfur, each the size of a small pea. *(10) What is the mass of the sulfur? (11) What is the volume occupied by the sulfur? (12) What is the mass of 1 cm^3 of sulfur?*

Concluding Questions

(1) Based on the results of this experiment, how do the properties of metals differ from those of nonmetals?

(2) Element X melts in boiling water; it fails to react with hydrochloric acid; and 1 cm^3 of element X has a mass of 1.8 g. Is element X a metal or a nonmetal? Give the reasons for your answer.

17 Physical and Chemical Properties of Two Metals – Magnesium and Copper

Purpose

To observe and identify physical and chemical properties of magnesium and copper.

Introduction

Physical properties are properties which can be determined without changing the composition of a substance. Chemical properties are those properties which can be determined when a change in composition of a substance occurs.

Physical changes involve changes in physical properties such as shape or state, with no new substances being formed. Chemical changes involve changes in composition and therefore the formation of new substances.

In this experiment you will determine and compare the physical and chemical properties of magnesium and copper.

Apparatus

crucible tongs
150 mm test tubes (8)
10 mL graduated cylinder

burner
medicine dropper

Materials

magnesium ribbon
copper wire
6 mol/L nitric acid

0.1% phenolphthalein solution
6 mol/L hydrochloric acid
steel wool

Procedure

A. Prepare a data table as shown. Record all experimental observations in the data table as soon as you obtain them.

Data Table 17-1

Part	Observations (Magnesium)	Observations (Copper)
B		
C		
D		
E		
F		
G		
H		
I		

B. Examine a piece of magnesium ribbon.

C. Attempt to bend a piece of magnesium ribbon.

D. Obtain two 3 cm pieces of magnesium. Clean the surface of each with a piece of steel wool.

E. Place one of the pieces of magnesium ribbon from part D into a test tube containing 3 mL of water. Add 2 drops of phenolphthalein solution and shake for 30 s.

F. Using crucible tongs, hold the other piece of magnesium ribbon in a burner flame to ignite the magnesium. **CAUTION: Do not look directly at the burning magnesium.** Remove the burning magnesium from the flame and allow it to continue to burn. Save the ignition product for part G.

G. Place the ignition product from part F into a test tube containing 3 mL of water. Add 2 drops of phenolphthalein indicator and shake for 30 s.

H. Add a 1 cm piece of magnesium ribbon to a test tube containing 1 mL of 6 mol/L hydrochloric acid and observe for 30 s.

I. Add a 1 cm piece of magnesium ribbon to a test tube containing 1 mL of 6 mol/L nitric acid and observe for 5 min.

J. Repeat parts B to I using copper wire in place of magnesium ribbon and record all observations in the data table.

Concluding Questions

(1) What types of evidence helped you decide whether you were observing a physical or a chemical property?

(2) What types of evidence helped you decide whether you were observing a physical or a chemical change?

(3) What are the similarities and differences in physical properties of magnesium and copper?

(4) What are the similarities and differences in chemical properties of magnesium and copper?

(5) Which property enables magnesium to be used in flashbulbs for photography?

18 The Variation of Atomic Properties

Purpose

To determine whether there is any regular variation in the properties of elements when the elements are arranged in order of increasing atomic number.

Introduction

In this exercise, you will plot two properties (atomic radius and first ionization energy) against the atomic numbers of the elements. You will examine the graphs in an attempt to find out whether there are any regular variations in the properties.

An atom does not have a definite boundary which determines its size. Nevertheless, there are techniques that make it possible to determine the distances between atoms in molecules. These distances can be used to devise a table of atomic radii which give fairly good approximations of the relative sizes of atoms. Thus, each atom can be thought of as a sphere having a specific radius.

The first ionization energy is the energy required to remove the first electron from an atom, M, in the gas phase as shown in the equation

$$M(g) \rightarrow M^+(g) + 1e^-$$

If the ionization energy is large, the electron must have been tightly held to the atom. For each element, the energy required to remove one electron from each atom in a mole of atoms is listed in the table.

Procedure

A. Plot atomic radius against atomic number. The data are given in Table 18-1.

Table 18-1 Atomic Properties

Atomic Number	Element	Atomic Radius (nm)	First Ionization Energy (kJ/mol of atoms)
1	H	0.032	1312
2	He	0.031	2372
3	Li	0.123	520
4	Be	0.090	899
5	B	0.082	801
6	C	0.077	1086
7	N	0.075	1402
8	O	0.073	1314
9	F	0.072	1681
10	Ne	0.071	2081
11	Na	0.154	496
12	Mg	0.136	738
13	Al	0.118	578
14	Si	0.111	786
15	P	0.106	1012
16	S	0.102	1000
17	Cl	0.099	1251
18	Ar	0.098	1521
19	K	0.203	419
20	Ca	0.174	590
21	Sc	0.144	631
22	Ti	0.132	658
23	V	0.122	650
24	Cr	0.118	653
25	Mn	—	—
26	Fe	0.117	759
27	Co	0.116	758
28	Ni	0.115	737
29	Cu	0.117	745
30	Zn	0.125	906
31	Ga	0.126	579
32	Ge	0.122	762
33	As	0.120	947
34	Se	—	—
35	Br	0.114	1140
36	Kr	0.112	1351

Design the scales for your graph on the graph paper provided. Divide the vertical axis into intervals of convenient size so that the largest atomic radius will appear near the top of the axis. Label the vertical axis *Atomic Radius.* Divide the horizontal axis into 36 intervals using as much of the axis as possible. Label this axis *Atomic Number.* Plot the datum for each element. Join consecutive points with solid straight lines. When the datum for an element is missing, use a broken straight line to join the points for the adjacent elements. *(1) How does the portion of the graph for elements 3 to 10 compare with the portion of the graph for elements 11 to 18? (2) How does the portion of the graph for elements 19 to 36 compare with the portion of the graph for elements 11 to 18? (3) If the data for the transition metals were missing and the data for elements 20 and 31 were joined directly with a broken line, how would the portion of the graph for elements 19 to 36 then compare with the portion of the graph for elements 11 to 18? (4) If there is a periodic variation (i.e., regular repetition) between atomic radii and atomic numbers of the elements, how would you describe it?*

B. Repeat part A, plotting first ionization energy against atomic number. These data are also given in Table 18-1. Label the vertical axis *First Ionization Energy.* *(5) How does the portion of the graph for elements 3 to 10 compare with the portion of the graph for elements 11 to 18? (6) How does the portion of the graph for elements 19 to 36 compare with the portion of the graph for elements 11 to 18? (7) If the data for the transition metals were missing and the data for elements 20 and 31 were joined directly with a broken line, how would the portion of the graph for elements 19 to 36 then compare with the portion of the graph for elements 11 to 18? (8) If there is a periodic variation between first ionization energy and atomic numbers of the elements, how would you describe it?*

Concluding Questions

(1) What do you estimate to be the missing value for the atomic radius of manganese? Of selenium?

(2) What do you estimate to be the missing value for the first ionization energy of manganese? Of selenium?

(3) Would you expect the atomic radius to be larger or smaller for element 37 than for element 36? Give the reason for your answer.

(4) What should be the approximate value for the first ionization energy of element 37?

(5) Which one of all the elements whose atomic numbers are larger than 36 should have the largest first ionization energy, and what will be the approximate value of its first ionization energy?

19 Hydrogen Chloride – A Molecule with a Polar Covalent Bond

Purpose

To prepare hydrogen chloride and to investigate the properties of a solution of hydrogen chloride in water.

Introduction

Hydrogen chloride gas (HCl) can be prepared by reacting an acid such as sulfuric acid (H_2SO_4) with a chloride such as sodium chloride (NaCl). In this experiment you will use concentrated sulfuric acid. CAUTION: Concentrated sulfuric acid is very corrosive to skin and clothing, and hydrogen chloride is very irritating to the mucous membranes. Do not prepare more hydrogen chloride than is absolutely necessary.

Apparatus

200 mm test tube
one-hole rubber stopper
   containing a bent glass tube
rubber tubing
50 mL graduated cylinder
funnel (65 mm diameter)
150 mm test tubes (8)

ring stand
burner
buret clamp
600 mL beakers (2)
stirring rod
watch glass

Materials

sodium chloride
12 mol/L sulfuric acid
red litmus paper

blue litmus paper
magnesium ribbon
iron filings

mossy zinc   calcium carbonate
copper wire   0.1 mol/L sodium chloride
0.1 mol/L silver nitrate

Procedure

A.   Place 30 mL of distilled water in each of two 600 mL beakers and assemble the apparatus as shown in Fig. 19-1.

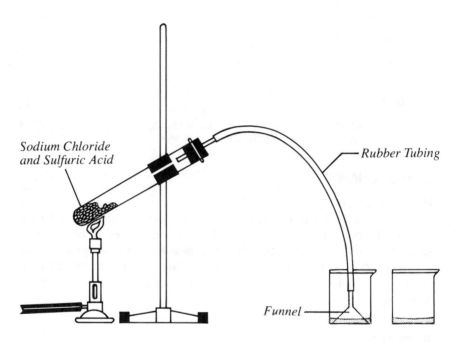

Fig. 19-1 Apparatus for the Preparation of Hydrogen Chloride

B.   Place 5 g of sodium chloride in a 200 mm test tube and add 10 mL of sulfuric acid. Attach the rubber stopper to the test tube immediately. Warm the test tube *gently* for 5 min, allowing the hydrogen chloride gas to pass into the 600 mL beaker. If vigorous bubbling occurs in the test tube, remove the heat to allow the reaction to slow down. *(1) Is there any evidence that the hydrogen chloride is dissolving in the water? (2) What physical properties of hydrogen chloride have you observed?*

C.   After 5 min of gentle heating, remove the funnel from the first beaker and place it in the second 600 mL beaker containing 30 mL of water. This will prevent any excess hydrogen chloride from escaping into the air. Turn off the burner. Retain the liquid in the first beaker for use in parts D, E, F, and G.

D. With a stirring rod, transfer 1 drop of distilled water to a piece of blue litmus paper and a second drop to a piece of red litmus paper, both placed on a watch glass. *(3) What do you observe?* Repeat this procedure with the liquid from part C. *(4) What do you observe?*

E. Place 5 mL of the liquid prepared in part B in each of four test tubes. To one of these test tubes add a small piece of magnesium ribbon. To a second test tube add some iron filings. To a third test tube add a piece of mossy zinc. Finally, add a small piece of copper wire to the fourth test tube. *(5) Does the liquid have any effect on magnesium, iron, zinc, or copper? (6) In which test tube does the liquid have the greatest effect? The least effect?*

F. To 5 mL of distilled water in a test tube, add 4 drops of silver nitrate solution. *(7) What do you observe?* To 5 mL of the liquid prepared in part C, add 4 drops of silver nitrate. *(8) What do you observe?* To 5 mL of sodium chloride solution, add 4 drops of silver nitrate. *(9) What do you observe?*

G. Pour the remainder of the liquid prepared in part C into a test tube. Add a marble chip (calcium carbonate). *(10) What do you observe?* Hold a lighted wooden splint in the mouth of this test tube. *(11) What do you observe?*

Concluding Questions

(1) What can you say about the solubility of hydrogen chloride in water?

(2) What chemical evidence do you have that the hydrogen chloride gas dissolved in water?

(3) From your experiment, what chemical property do aqueous solutions of hydrogen chloride and sodium chloride have in common? Why do you suppose this is so?

20 Carbon Dioxide — A Double-Bonded Molecule

Purpose

To prepare carbon dioxide and examine some of its properties.

Introduction

In this experiment carbon dioxide is prepared by reacting calcium carbonate with hydrochloric acid. The products are calcium chloride, water, and carbon dioxide. The carbon dioxide is collected by the displacement of water.

Apparatus

250 mL Florence flask
two-hole rubber stopper
bent glass tube (60°)
250 mL beaker
125 mL wide-mouth bottles (2)
pneumatic trough
buret clamp
rubber stoppers (2)

thistle tube
burner
rubber tubing
ring stand
glass squares (2)
deflagrating spoon
150 mm test tubes (5)

Materials

calcium carbonate chips
6 mol/L hydrochloric acid
wooden splint
limewater
0.1 mol/L sodium hydroxide

red litmus paper
blue litmus paper
candle
magnesium ribbon
phenolphthalein

Procedure

A. Place 50 g of calcium carbonate chips in an empty 250 mL Florence or Erlenmeyer flask. A flask containing 50 g of chips is on display for comparison. Cover the calcium carbonate chips with water.

B. Set up the apparatus for the preparation and collection of carbon dioxide as in Fig. 20-1. Place two water-filled, wide-mouth bottles and two water-filled, 150 mm test tubes upside down in a trough of water.

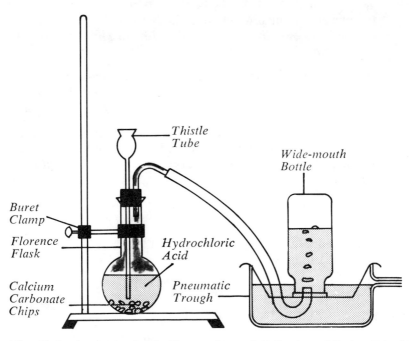

Fig. 20-1 Apparatus for the Preparation and Collection of Carbon Dioxide

C. Carefully add hydrochloric acid to the calcium carbonate a little at a time to maintain a constant evolution of gas for 15 s. Do not collect this gas. *(1) Why isn't this initial gas collected?* After 15 s begin to collect the gas. Add hydrochloric acid as needed. Collect two bottles and two test tubes of carbon dioxide gas. After the gas has been collected, cover the bottles with glass squares and stopper the test tubes. *(2) Is carbon dioxide very soluble in water? How do you know?*

D. Wind the end of a 5 cm piece of magnesium ribbon around the bottom of a deflagrating spoon. Light the other end of the magnesium ribbon in your Bunsen burner flame. **CAUTION: Do not look directly at the burning magnesium.** Quickly lower the burning magnesium into a bottle of carbon dioxide, being careful not to touch the bottle with the magnesium. *(3) What do you observe?*

E. Light a wooden splint and thrust it into a test tube of carbon dioxide. *(4) What do you observe?*

F. Place a short candle in a 250 mL beaker and light it. Place a bottle of carbon dioxide just above the beaker. Tilt the bottle *as if* you were pouring water from the bottle onto the candle. Be careful not to pour any residual water from the bottle onto the flames of the candle. *(5) What do you observe? (6) What physical property of carbon dioxide is demonstrated?*

G. Allow carbon dioxide from the generator to bubble through 5 mL of limewater contained in a test tube until you notice a change. The result is a test for carbon dioxide. *(7) What is the result?*

H. In a test tube place 5 mL of 0.1 mol/L sodium hydroxide and 2 drops of phenolphthalein. Allow carbon dioxide from the generator to bubble through the solution for 2 min. *(8) What do you observe?*

I. Place moistened pieces of red and blue litmus papers into the second test tube of carbon dioxide. *(9) What is the result?*

J. Place about 10 mL of limewater in a test tube. Exhale into the tube for 1 min. Stopper the test tube and shake. *(10) What is the result?*

Concluding Questions

(1) Was there any evidence that carbon dioxide had decomposed in part D? In part E?

(2) Is carbon dioxide a stable molecule? What evidence do you have to support your answer?

(3) What do the results of part J show?

(4) From this experiment, what are some physical properties of carbon dioxide?

(5) From this experiment, what are some chemical properties of carbon dioxide?

(6) From this experiment, what are some chemical properties of a solution of carbon dioxide in water?

21 Physical Properties of Two Types of Solids

Purpose

To study some of the physical properties of two types of solids — molecular and ionic.

Introduction

Some solids consist of molecules in which the atoms are held together by covalent bonds. The molecules are held together by van der Waals forces of attraction. These solids are called molecular solids.

Other solids consist of an array of positive and negative ions, arranged in such a way that every positive ion has only negative neighbours and vice versa. The solid is held together because of the attractions between ions of opposite charge. Such solids are called ionic solids.

In this experiment, you will examine four physical properties (odour, hardness, melting point, and solubility) of a molecular and an ionic solid. You will attempt to relate these properties to the forces of attraction between the particles in each solid. The solids are sodium chloride and camphor. Camphor contains carbon, hydrogen, and oxygen.

Apparatus

filter paper	iron ring
watch glass	ring stand
Scoopula®	burner
crucible cover	150 mm test tubes (4)
clay triangle	10 mL graduated cylinder

Materials

sodium chloride   2-propanol
camphor

Procedure

A. Prepare a data table as shown. Record all experimental results as
soon as you obtain them.

Data Table 21-1

Physical Property	Sodium Chloride	Camphor
Odour (strong, weak, or nil)		
Hardness (hard or soft)		
Melting point (high or low)		
Solubility in water (soluble or insoluble)		
Solubility in 2-propanol (soluble or insoluble)		

B. On 2 pieces of filter paper place separate 0.2 g samples of sodium
chloride and camphor. Observe the odour of each solid.

C. Rub a small sample of each solid between your fingers. Note
whether each feels soft or hard. Check by attempting to crush a
few small crystals of each solid between a Scoopula® and a watch
glass.

D. Place a few crystals of sodium chloride and camphor side by side
in separate piles on an inverted crucible cover. Support the
crucible cover on a clay triangle on an iron ring and heat it gently
until one of the two solids melts. Then heat the crucible cover
more strongly for a few minutes. The molten solid will probably
catch fire and burn with a smoky flame. (For this reason, only a
few crystals of each solid should be used.) *(1) Does the second
solid melt at the higher temperatures reached by the burner?*

E. Divide the remaining crystals of sodium chloride evenly between
two test tubes. Divide the remaining crystals of camphor between

two other test tubes. You should have nearly 0.1 g of solid in each test tube. To one test tube containing sodium chloride add 3 mL of water and shake vigorously. To one test tube containing camphor add 3 mL of water and shake vigorously. To each of the two remaining test tubes add 3 mL of 2-propanol and shake vigorously.

Concluding Questions

(1) On the basis of the electronegativities of sodium, chlorine, carbon, hydrogen, and oxygen, which substance is the ionic solid?

(2) What does a strong odour indicate about the ease with which the particles in a solid leave its surface?

(3) From your answers to questions 1 and 2 and your observations of odour, which of the two types of solids seems to have the stronger forces of attraction? Explain your answer.

(4) From your observations of hardness and melting points, how does the strength of van der Waals forces of attraction compare with the strength of the attractions between ions of opposite charge?

(5) Water is a much more polar molecule than 2-propanol. How does the polarity of the liquid seem to influence the solubilities of these two solids?

22 Preparation of an Alloy

Purpose

To prepare the alloy, brass.

Introduction

An alloy is a substance which has metallic properties and which contains more than one element. Alloys are made because they have desirable properties. For example, stainless steel is mainly iron, but, whereas iron corrodes rapidly, stainless steel resists corrosion. In this experiment you will prepare brass, an alloy of copper and zinc. Brass has the desirable property of resisting corrosion and is used in marine hardware.

Apparatus

250 mL beaker	iron ring	wire gauze
ring stand	crucible tongs	watch glass
burner		

Materials

zinc powder	3 mol/L sodium hydroxide
copper wire	various copper items
steel wool	

Procedure

A. Obtain about 1 g of zinc powder and place it on the bottom of a 250 mL beaker. Add 50 mL of a 3 mol/L sodium hydroxide solution.

B. Place a watch glass on top of the beaker and heat the solution until it starts to boil. Turn off the burner. Clean a piece of copper wire with steel wool. Place the piece of copper wire into the bottom of the beaker so that it is covered completely by the sodium hydroxide solution. Allow the copper wire to remain in the solution for 6 min. *(1) What do you observe in the beaker during the 6 min?*

C. After 6 min remove the copper wire from the beaker with a pair of crucible tongs. Wash this wire, ensuring that any pieces of zinc adhering to it are removed. Dry it by blotting it with a paper towel. *(2) How has the copper wire changed?*

D. Half-fill a beaker with water. Hold the copper wire from part C with a pair of crucible tongs and place the wire in the outer, cooler flame of your burner. As soon as the wire begins to turn yellow, wait about 1 s, quickly remove the wire from the flame, and plunge it in the beaker of water. Wash the wire and blot it dry with a paper towel. *(3) What do you observe?*

E. Cut the wire from part D in half and examine a cross section of it. *(4) What do you observe?*

F. Use steel wool to clean the copper items that you have brought from home. Place them in the beaker containing the zinc powder and sodium hydroxide solution. Cover the beaker with a watch glass and then heat the solution until it begins to boil. Turn off the burner and allow the copper items to remain in the solution for 6 min. Then follow the procedure of parts C and D. After the copper items have been removed from the beaker, decant the sodium hydroxide solution; rinse the zinc residue with water; and dispose of the residue as directed by your teacher.

Concluding Questions

(1) What is the substance on the surface of the copper wire at the end of part B?

(2) Why is the wire in part C dried by blotting it gently with a paper towel rather than by rubbing it vigorously?

(3) What is the substance formed on the surface of the copper wire in part D as a result of the heating of the wire?

(4) How do you suppose this substance was formed?

(5) What do the observations of part E indicate?

(6) Why do you suppose that the wire should not be left too long in the burner flame in part D?

23 The Degree of Saturation of a Solution

Purpose

To prepare aqueous solutions of sodium acetate with different degrees of saturation and to study the properties of these solutions.

Introduction

Three possibilities can exist when a solute is dissolved in a given amount of solvent. The resulting solution can be unsaturated (contain less solute than the solvent is capable of holding); or it can be saturated (contain the maximum amount of solute that the solvent is capable of holding); or it can be supersaturated (contain more than the maximum amount of solute that the solvent is capable of holding under the given conditions).

In this experiment, you will prepare solutions of each type, identify them, and study some of their properties.

Apparatus

150 mm test tubes (2)
cork stopper
test tube holder
burner
250 mL beaker

Materials

hydrated sodium acetate

Procedure

A.   Place 5 mL of water in a 150 mm test tube. Add a few milligrams (a few tiny crystals) of hydrated sodium acetate and shake vigorously. *(1) What do you observe?* Add a few more crystals and shake again. *(2) What do you observe?*

B.   Now add 3.5 g of hydrated sodium acetate to the solution. Stopper the test tube with a cork and shake vigorously for 1 min. *(3) What do you observe?* Allow the test tube to rest at an angle for a minute to promote faster settling of any suspended matter, then pour the clear upper liquid into a *dry* test tube. To the clear liquid add a few milligrams of sodium acetate and shake vigorously for 1 min. *(4) What do you observe?*

C.   Pour the contents of the second test tube back into the first tube and add an extra 3.0 g of hydrated sodium acetate. The added solid usually forms a plug just above the surface of the liquid. Holding the tube in a nearly horizontal position and taking care not to point the open end at anyone, heat the liquid gently to dissolve this plug partially. Then hold the tube in a nearly upright position and heat the liquid from the top to the bottom in order to bring the liquid to a gentle boil and dissolve all the crystals. Avoid "bumping" (sudden, irregular bubbling), which becomes more serious once all the crystals have disappeared.

D.   Gently place the test tube in a beaker of cold water and allow it to remain undisturbed for 5 min. If crystals appear at any point, remove the test tube, reheat it gently to redissolve the crystals, and place the test tube in water for another 5 min. Gently remove the test tube and add one or two tiny crystals of sodium acetate. *(5) What do you observe?*

Concluding Questions

(1)   What kind of solution did you have in part A? How do you know?

(2)   What kind of solution was the clear liquid that you added to the second test tube in part B? How do you know?

(3)   Why did your second test tube have to be dry?

(4)   What kind of solution did you have in part D before the crystals of sodium acetate were added? How do you know?

(5)   What kind of solution did you have after the crystals were added?

(6) What happens when a small particle of solute is added to an unsaturated solution? Explain.

(7) What happens when a small particle of solute is added to a saturated solution? Explain.

(8) What happens when a small particle of solute is added to a supersaturated solution? Explain.

24 Solutions and Molecular Polarity

Purpose

To study the effects of molecular polarity on the solubility of a substance in a liquid solvent and to determine whether an unknown substance is nonpolar, polar, or ionic.

Introduction

Most people know that sugar dissolves in some liquids but not in others. What factors determine whether one substance will dissolve in another? The solubility of one substance in another depends on the nature of the two substances involved. For example, there are attractive forces between the molecules of sugar in a sugar crystal, and there are attractive forces between the water molecules in pure water. In order for sugar to dissolve in water, the water must be able to overcome the attractive forces that the sugar molecules have for each other, and the sugar must be able to overcome the attractive forces that the water molecules have for each other. This can be accomplished by the attraction between the sugar molecules and the water molecules. Thus, the polarities of the substance(s) being dissolved and the solvent are important in determining whether or not a solution will result.

In this experiment, you will attempt to dissolve nonpolar, polar, and ionic substances in solvents of different polarity. The solvents you will use are trichlorotrifluoroethane (almost nonpolar), ethanol (polar), and water (highly polar). You will use the results to determine whether an unknown substance is nonpolar, polar, or ionic, and you will formulate some principles concerning the effect of molecular polarity on solubility.

Apparatus

150 mm test tubes (12)   cork stoppers (3)

Materials

ethanol   ammonium chloride
trichlorotrifluoroethane (TTE)   glycerol
iodine   unknown solute

Procedure

A. Prepare a data table as shown. Record all experimental results in the data table as soon as you obtain them.

Data Table 24-1

Solubility	In Water	In Ethanol	In TTE
Of I_2 Of NH_4Cl Of glycerol Of unknown			

B. Use the diagram on the inside front cover of this laboratory manual as a guide in making all volume measurements in this experiment. Place 5 mL of water, ethanol, and TTE separately in three test tubes. To each of the three test tubes add two small iodine crystals. Stopper the test tubes and shake well. Observe the contents of each tube carefully to determine whether the iodine has dissolved. *(1) In which type of solvent is iodine most soluble?*

C. Pour separately into three more test tubes 5 mL volumes of water, ethanol, and TTE. To each of the test tubes add two small crystals of ammonium chloride. Stopper the test tubes and shake vigorously. Observe the contents of each tube carefully to determine whether the ammonium chloride has dissolved. *(2) In which type of solvent is ammonium chloride most soluble?*

D. Repeat the procedure of part C, using 2 drops of glycerol instead of the 2 crystals of ammonium chloride. *(3) In which type of solvent is glycerol most soluble?*

E. Obtain an unknown from your teacher. Use the procedure of part C to determine the solubility of two small crystals (if your unknown is a solid) or 2 drops (if your unknown is a liquid) of your unknown. *(4) In which type of solvent is your unknown most soluble?*

Concluding Questions

(1) From your knowledge of the periodic table, electronegativities, and bond types, would you say that iodine molecules are nonpolar, polar, or ionic?

(2) How do you explain the differences you observed between the solubilities of iodine in water and in TTE?

(3) Is ammonium chloride a nonpolar, polar, or ionic substance?

(4) How do you explain, in terms of molecular polarities, the differences you observed between the solubilities of ammonium chloride in water and in TTE?

(5) Is glycerol a nonpolar, polar, or ionic substance?

(6) How do you explain, in terms of molecular polarities, the differences you observe among the solubilities of glycerol in the three solvents?

(7) Is your unknown a nonpolar, polar, or ionic substance? How do you know?

(8) In what type of solvent is an ionic substance most soluble?

(9) In what type of solvent is a polar substance most soluble?

(10) In what type of solvent is a nonpolar substance most soluble?

(11) What generalized statement, if any, can you make summarizing the effect of bond polarity on the solubility of a substance in a solvent?

(12) When water and chloroform are mixed, the components separate into two layers, each of which smells strongly of chloroform. How would you quickly and easily confirm which layer is mainly water and which is mainly chloroform?

25 Acids and Bases

Purpose

To discover some of the properties of acids and bases.

Introduction

Acids ionize in water, producing hydronium ions (H_3O^+) and various negative ions. For example, nitric acid ionizes in water to produce hydronium ions and nitrate ions. Bases produce hydroxide ions (OH^-) and various positive ions when they are dissolved in water. For example, potassium hydroxide produces potassium ions and hydroxide ions when it is dissolved in water.

The pH scale can be used to assess the acidity or basicity of a solution. Acidic solutions have pH values below seven. The further below seven the pH is, the more acidic the solution is. Basic solutions have pH values above seven. The further above seven the pH is, the more basic the solution is.

Acid-base indicators are substances which change colour over different pH ranges. Methyl orange is red below pH 3.1 and orange-yellow above pH 4.4. Indigo carmine is blue in all solutions having a pH below 11.6, but it is yellow in solutions having a pH above 13. Phenolphthalein is colourless below pH 8.2 and turns pink above 8.2.

We will use this information regarding the pH scale and acid-base indicators to discover some properties of acids and bases.

Apparatus

watch glass	10 mL graduated cylinder
stirring rods (2)	medicine dropper
150 mm test tubes (7)	

Materials

red litmus paper	methyl orange solution
blue litmus paper	indigo carmine solution
0.1 mol/L hydrochloric acid	mossy zinc
0.1 mol/L sodium hydroxide	6 mol/L hydrochloric acid
0.1 mol/L acetic acid	6 mol/L acetic acid
0.1 mol/L ammonia water	phenolphthalein solution

Procedure

A. Place a piece of red litmus paper and a piece of blue litmus paper on a watch glass. Using a stirring rod, transfer 1 drop of 0.1 mol/L hydrochloric acid to one end of the piece of red litmus paper, and transfer a second drop to one end of the piece of blue litmus paper. *(1) What do you observe?* Now use another stirring rod to transfer 1 drop of 0.1 mol/L sodium hydroxide to the other end (the dry end) of the piece of red litmus paper, and transfer a second drop to the other end of the piece of blue litmus paper. *(2) What do you observe?*

B. Add 2 mL of 0.1 mol/L hydrochloric acid to a test tube containing 5 mL of water. Add 1 drop of methyl orange indicator. Mix the solution. *(3) What do you observe?* Repeat, using 0.1 mol/L acetic acid in place of the hydrochloric acid. *(4) What do you observe?*

C. Place 5 mL of 0.1 mol/L sodium hydroxide in a test tube. Add 2 drops of indigo carmine indicator and mix the liquid in the test tube. *(5) What do you observe?* Repeat, using 0.1 mol/L ammonia water. *(6) What do you observe?*

D. Add 1 mL of 0.1 mol/L sodium hydroxide to 9 mL of water to form 0.01 mol/L sodium hydroxide. Add 2 drops of indigo carmine solution to 5 mL of the 0.01 mol/L sodium hydroxide and mix the liquid in the test tube. *(7) Is the colour of the indigo carmine the same as it was when you tested 0.1 mol/L sodium hydroxide?* Add 1 mL of 0.01 mol/L sodium hydroxide to 9 mL of water to form 0.001 mol/L sodium hydroxide. Add 2 drops of indigo carmine solution to 5 mL of the 0.001 mol/L sodium hydroxide and mix the liquid in the test tube. *(8) Is the colour of the indigo carmine the same as it was when you tested 0.01 mol/L sodium hydroxide?*

E. Place a small piece of mossy zinc in each of two test tubes. To the first test tube add 5 mL of 6 mol/L hydrochloric acid. *(9) What do you observe?* To the second test tube add 5 mL of 6 mol/L acetic acid. *(10) What do you observe? (11) In which test tube is the reaction more vigorous?*

F. Using a clean medicine dropper, place 20 drops of 0.1 mol/L hydrochloric acid in a test tube. Add 1 drop of phenolphthalein solution to the test tube. Rinse the dropper with water and add 0.1 mol/L sodium hydroxide one drop at a time to the hydrochloric acid solution until you observe a change. *(12) What change do you observe? (13) What does this change indicate? (14) How many drops of sodium hydroxide were required to bring about the change?*

Concluding Questions

(1) For what purpose can litmus paper be used?

(2) In part B, do solutions of hydrochloric acid and acetic acid (both having the same concentration) appear to contain the same quantity of hydronium ions per unit volume?

(3) In part C, do solutions of sodium hydroxide and ammonia water (both having the same concentration) appear to contain the same quantity of hydroxide ions per unit volume?

(4) In part D, what effect does diluting the sodium hydroxide have on the basicity of the solution?

(5) In part E, the zinc reacted with hydronium ions from the acid to produce hydrogen gas. Do the results of part E confirm your answer to Concluding Question 2?

(6) Commercial vinegar is a solution of acetic acid in water. How would you determine which brand of vinegar contains more acetic acid in a given volume of vinegar?

26 Identification of Solutions

Purpose

To identify five solutions.

Introduction

In this experiment, you are asked to identify the following solutions:

0.1 mol/L H_2SO_4 0.1 mol/L NaOH

0.1 mol/L $Ba(OH)_2$ 0.1 mol/L Na_2SO_4

0.1 mol/L $Pb(NO_3)_2$

    The solutions are dispensed in coded test tubes. Your only tool for identification of the solution present in each test tube is a solution of methyl orange, an indicator which is pinkish-red in acid solution and yellowish-orange in neutral and basic solution. Of the five unknown solutions, only the sulfuric acid is acidic enough to turn the methyl orange pinkish-red. Sodium hydroxide and barium hydroxide are basic, and sodium sulfate and lead nitrate are neutral salts. If you add methyl orange to 5 mL of each separate solution, you should be able to identify the sulfuric acid.

    You can now use the sulfuric acid to test the other four solutions. Sulfuric acid will cause the formation of a precipitate of lead (II) sulfate to form when it is added to a solution of lead (II) nitrate. The solution will still be acidic because nitric acid is formed. Sulfuric acid will cause the formation of a precipitate of barium sulfate when it is added to barium hydroxide. The solution will no longer be acidic because the base (barium hydroxide) is neutralized by the sulfuric acid to form the precipitate and water.

    Sulfuric acid does not react with sodium sulfate. There will be no precipitate and the solution will still be acidic because of the sulfuric acid. Sulfuric acid is neutralized by the sodium hydroxide but no precipitate is formed. The solution is not acidic because both the sodium sulfate and the water formed are neutral.

Apparatus

150 mm test tubes (5)

Materials

1 set of solutions in coded test tubes
methyl orange solution

Procedure

A. Using the chart on the inside front cover of this manual as a guide, pour 5 mL of each unknown solution into separate test tubes. Add 2 drops of methyl orange solution to each test tube. *(1) Which test tube contains the sulfuric acid?*

B. Add 1 mL of the sulfuric acid to each of the four remaining test tubes which contain 5 mL of solution and 2 drops of methyl orange. Observe the colour of the solution and note the presence or absence of a precipitate in each test tube.

Concluding Questions

(1) Which test tube contains the barium hydroxide? How do you know?

(2) Which test tube contains the lead nitrate? How do you know?

(3) Which test tube contains the sodium sulfate? How do you know?

(4) Which test tube contains the sodium hydroxide? How do you know?

27 Solutions and Solubility

Purpose

To identify six unknown solutions.

Introduction

In this experiment you are asked to identify six solutions. The solutions are

0.1 mol/L $CuSO_4$	0.1 mol/L Na_2CO_3
0.1 mol/L $Cu(NO_3)_2$	0.1 mol/L $(NH_4)_2SO_4$
0.1 mol/L $BaCl_2$	0.1 mol/L $ZnSO_4$

The solutions are dispensed in coded test tubes. Your major tool for identifying the solutions will be the following information:

(i)   All nitrates are soluble.

(ii)   Nearly all compounds of lithium, sodium, potassium, and ammonium are soluble.

(iii) Nearly all chlorides are soluble except for $AgCl$, Hg_2Cl_2, and $PbCl_2$.

(iv) Nearly all sulfates are soluble except for $CaSO_4$, $BaSO_4$, $SrSO_4$, and $PbSO_4$.

(v)   Nearly all carbonates are insoluble; however, Li_2CO_3, Na_2CO_3, K_2CO_3, and $(NH_4)_2CO_3$ are soluble.

(vi) In addition, copper(II) ions are blue, while all other ions in the unknown solutions are colourless.

There are many ways to identify the six solutions. One suggestion is given in the experimental procedure.

Apparatus

150 mm test tubes (14)

Materials

1 set of solutions in coded test tubes

Procedure

A. Using the chart on the inside front cover of this manual as a guide, transfer 10 mL of each solution from the coded test tubes to similarly labelled test tubes in your test tube rack. Use only a small portion of each unknown solution in any one test.

B. Identify the copper solutions by their colour. *(1) Which two coded test tubes contain copper solutions?*

C. Using the chart on the inside front cover of this manual as a guide, add 1 mL of each copper solution to 1 mL of each of the other four unknown solutions, all in separate test tubes. *(Note:* A total of eight test tubes will be used.) Observe whether or not a precipitate forms in each case. *(2) Which mixtures of solutions produce precipitates?*

D. To help you identify $CuSO_4$, $Cu(NO_3)_2$, $BaCl_2$, and Na_2CO_3 solutions, note the following:
   (i) When $CuSO_4$ solution is added to each of the four solutions, precipitates will form with $BaCl_2$ and Na_2CO_3. The precipitates are barium sulfate and copper(II) carbonate, respectively.
   (ii) When $Cu(NO_3)_2$ is added to each of the four solutions, a precipitate will form only with Na_2CO_3. The precipitate is copper(II) carbonate.
   (3) Which test tube contains $CuSO_4$? (4) Which test tube contains $Cu(NO_3)_2$? (5) Which test tube contains Na_2CO_3? (6) Which test tube contains $BaCl_2$?

E. Devise a method to identify the ammonium sulfate, $(NH_4)_2SO_4$, and the zinc sulfate, $ZnSO_4$. *(7) What method did you use to distinguish between the $(NH_4)_2SO_4$ and the $ZnSO_4$? (8) Which test tube contains $(NH_4)_2SO_4$? (9) Which test tube contains $ZnSO_4$?*

28 Forming Precipitates and Balancing Equations

Purpose

To prepare several precipitates and to balance the chemical equations for the reactions involved.

Introduction

Many compounds dissolve in water — they are soluble in water. However, other compounds are insoluble in water. An insoluble solid product of a chemical reaction which is occurring in solution is called a precipitate. One example of an insoluble compound is silver chloride. Silver nitrate and sodium chloride both dissolve in water, but when a solution of silver nitrate is mixed with a solution of sodium chloride, one of the products (silver chloride) is insoluble in water. The silver chloride forms a precipitate which falls to the bottom of the reaction container. The other product (sodium nitrate) remains dissolved.

Chemists generally do not like to write a paragraph to describe a chemical process if they can do it just as well in one line. A chemical equation is a convenient way of describing a chemical reaction. In the case of the preceding example, the chemical equation is

$$AgNO_3(aq) + NaCl(aq) \rightarrow AgCl(s) + NaNO_3(aq)$$

This equation tells us that a solution of silver nitrate in water can be mixed with a solution of sodium chloride in water to form a solid precipitate of silver chloride and a solution of sodium nitrate in water. A reaction such as this, which involves a joint exchange of partners, is called a double displacement reaction.

The formation of precipitates is frequently used by chemists in analytical work. For example, if a substance contains an unknown quantity of sulfate ions, the substance is first dissolved in water and

87

then a reagent such as barium chloride is added to the solution. A precipitate of barium sulfate forms. Essentially all of the sulfate ions present in the substance are removed from the solution as the barium sulfate precipitate forms. The quantity of barium sulfate precipitate can be determined, and this information leads to a calculation of the amount of sulfate which must have been present in the sample.

In this experiment, you will mix solutions of various compounds, describe and name the precipitates, and write balanced chemical equations for the reactions. The reactions that occur in this experiment are double displacement reactions.

Apparatus

100 mL beaker   150 mm test tubes (8)

Materials

iron(III) nitrate   sodium phosphate
iron(II) sulfate   lead nitrate
copper(II) sulfate   potassium iodide
0.1 mol/L sodium hydroxide   0.1 mol/L silver nitrate

Procedure

A. Place about 15 mL of 0.1 mol/L sodium hydroxide solution in a 100 mL beaker. *(1) What is the colour of this solution?* This reagent will be used in parts B, C, and D.

B. Dissolve a small quantity of powdered iron(III) nitrate (about the size of a match head) in water in a test tube. Use the smallest amount of water possible. *(2) What is the colour of the iron(III) nitrate solution?* In a second test tube place a matching volume of the sodium hydroxide solution. Mix the two solutions in the first test tube and observe the precipitate. *(3) What is the colour of the precipitate?*

C. Repeat part B using powdered iron(II) sulfate in place of the iron(III) nitrate. *(4) What is the colour of the iron(II) sulfate solution? (5) What is the colour of the precipitate?*

D. Repeat part B using powdered copper(II) sulfate in place of the iron(III) nitrate. *(6) What is the colour of the copper(II) sulfate solution? (7) What is the colour of the precipitate?*

E. Dissolve a small quantity of powdered sodium phosphate (about the size of a match head) in water in a test tube. Use the smallest amount of water possible. *(8) What is the colour of the sodium phosphate solution?* In another test tube place a matching volume of 0.1 mol/L silver nitrate solution. *(9) What is the colour of the silver nitrate solution?* Mix the two solutions in one of the test tubes and observe the precipitate. *(10) What is the colour of the precipitate?*

F. Dissolve small quantities of powdered lead nitrate and potassium iodide (about the size of a match head for each) in water in separate test tubes. Use the smallest amount of water possible in each case. *(11) What are the colours of the two solutions?* Mix the two solutions and observe the precipitate. *(12) What is the colour of the precipitate?*

Concluding Questions

(1) What are the balanced chemical equations for these precipitation reactions? (You must write correct chemical formulas for the compounds involved in these reactions; you must make sure that you have the same number of atoms of each element on both sides of the yields sign; and you must indicate which product is the precipitate in each equation. If you have difficulty with this last item, consult the table of solubility rules found at the end of this laboratory manual.)

(2) What does (aq) signify in a chemical equation?

(3) What does (s) signify in a chemical equation?

29 Types of Chemical Reactions

Purpose

To study four different types of chemical reactions.

Introduction

It is not easy to classify all chemical reactions precisely. Nevertheless, most reactions can be classified into one of four major categories.

Addition reactions, or *direct combinations*, are reactions in which atoms and molecules join together directly to produce larger molecules. An example of an addition reaction is the combustion of sulfur to form sulfur dioxide:

$$S + O_2 \rightarrow SO_2$$

Decomposition reactions are just the opposite of addition reactions. An example is the decomposition of carbonic acid:

$$H_2CO_3 \rightarrow H_2O + CO_2$$

Displacement or *substitution* reactions involve a change of partners. An example of a displacement reaction is the liberation of bromine from calcium bromide by the action of chlorine:

$$Cl_2 + CaBr_2 \rightarrow CaCl_2 + Br_2$$

Double displacement or *metathetic* reactions involve a joint exchange of partners, as in the precipitation of silver chloride when solutions of silver nitrate and sodium chloride are mixed:

$$AgNO_3 + NaCl \rightarrow AgCl + NaNO_3$$

In this experiment you will study six different chemical reactions. You will identify some of the products and then classify each reaction as one of the four types.

Apparatus

burner

crucible tongs

150 mm test tubes (5)

medicine dropper

10 mL graduated cylinder

test tube holder

Materials

wood splints

0.5 mol/L sodium sulfate

0.5 mol/L barium chloride

mossy zinc

3 mol/L hydrochloric acid

manganese dioxide

iron nail

0.3 mol/L copper(II) sulfate

copper wire

6% hydrogen peroxide

copper(II) sulfate pentahydrate

Procedure

A. Place about 0.25 g of copper(II) sulfate pentahydrate crystals (compared with a sample on display) in a clean, dry test tube and heat until no further change is observed. *(1) What do you observe on the upper part of the test tube? (2) What do you observe in the bottom of the test tube?* Allow the test tube to cool, and add 5 drops of water. *(3) What do you observe? (4) What is the substance remaining in the test tube after the heating?*

B. Place 5 mL of sodium sulfate solution in a test tube. Add a medicine dropper full of barium chloride solution. *(5) What do you observe? (6) If one of the products is sodium chloride (which is soluble in water), what is the other product?*

C. Using crucible tongs, hold a 5 cm piece of copper wire in a burner flame. Remove the wire and examine it. *(7) What do you observe? (8) With what did the copper combine?*

D. Place a small piece of mossy zinc in a test tube. Add 5 mL of dilute hydrochloric acid. *(9) What do you observe?*

E. Place 3 mL of hydrogen peroxide in a test tube. Add a pinch of manganese dioxide. *(10) What do you observe?* Insert a glowing splint into the mouth of the test tube. *(11) What do you observe?* Water is one product of this reaction. *(12) What is the other product of this reaction?*

F. Place a clean iron nail in a test tube and cover it with a solution of copper(II) sulfate. After several minutes, remove the nail and examine it. *(13) Do you observe any change in the appearance of the nail? (14) If so, what is the change? (15) Do you observe* *any change in the appearance of the copper(II) sulfate solution? (16) If so, what is the change?*

Concluding Questions

(1) What word equations describe the chemical reactions taking place in parts A to F?

(2) What type of chemical reaction is illustrated in each part of this experiment?

(3) What is the balanced chemical equation for each reaction taking place in parts A to F?

EXPERIMENT

30 Redox Reactions of Metals and Nonmetals

Purpose

(a) To arrange the metals copper, zinc, and lead in order of their relative abilities to donate electrons and to arrange the metal ions in order of their ability to accept electrons.

(b) To arrange the halogens bromine, chlorine, and iodine in order of their relative abilities to accept electrons and to arrange the halide ions in order of their ability to donate electrons.

Introduction

The loss of electrons from an atom, with a consequent increase in oxidation number, is called oxidation. The substance which loses electrons is said to be oxidized, and the substance which removes them is called the oxidizing agent.

The gain of electrons by an atom, with a consequent decrease in oxidation number, is called reduction. The substance which gains electrons is said to be reduced, and the substance which supplies them is called the reducing agent.

Oxidation-reduction reactions involve a competition of substances for electrons. Strong oxidizing agents have a strong tendency to accept electrons. Strong reducing agents have little attraction for the electrons they already possess. Thus, tin(II) ion is a stronger oxidizing agent than is nickel(II) ion because the reaction

$$Ni(s) + Sn^{2+}(aq) \rightarrow Ni^{2+}(aq) + Sn(s)$$

goes predominantly to the right. That is, tin ions have a greater ability to remove electrons than nickel ions. Also, nickel metal is a stronger reducing agent than is tin metal, because nickel releases its electrons more readily.

In this experiment you will perform tests with three metals and their ions. By noting which tests give positive results you will be able

93

to arrange the metals and their ions according to their relative abilities to donate and accept electrons. A similar series of tests with halogens will allow you to arrange the halogens and the halide ions according to their relative abilities to accept and donate electrons.

Apparatus

150 mm test tubes (6)

Materials

copper metal
zinc metal
lead metal
0.1 mol/L zinc(II) nitrate
0.1 mol/L lead(II) nitrate
0.1 mol/L copper(II) nitrate
trichlorotrifluoroethane (TTE)

chlorine water
bromine water
iodine solution
0.1 mol/L potassium bromide
0.1 mol/L potassium chloride
0.1 mol/L potassium iodide

Procedure

A. Using the chart on the inside front cover of this manual as a guide, place 3 mL of a solution of zinc(II) nitrate in a test tube. Add a small piece of copper metal. *(1) What do you observe?* Place a small piece of copper metal in 3 mL of a solution of lead(II) nitrate. *(2) What do you observe?*

B. Similarly, test the behaviour of small pieces of zinc metal in separate solutions of copper(II) nitrate and lead(II) nitrate. *(3) What do you observe in each case?*

C. Next, add small pieces of lead metal to separate 3 mL portions of copper(II) nitrate and zinc(II) nitrate. *(4) What do you observe in each case?*

D. In each of three test tubes, place 1 mL of TTE and 3 mL of water. *(5) What do you observe?* To one test tube add 5 drops of chlorine water and shake vigorously. *(6) What colour is a solution of chlorine in water? In TTE?* To a second test tube add 5 drops of bromine water and shake vigorously. *(7) What colour is a solution of bromine in water? In TTE? (8) In which solvent is the bromine more soluble?* To the third test tube add 5 drops of iodine solution and shake vigorously. *(9) What is the colour of a solution of iodine in water? In TTE? (10) In which solvent is the iodine more soluble?*

E. Test the behaviour of a 3 mL sample of potassium bromide solution with 1 mL of TTE when 5 drops of chlorine water are added and shaken vigorously. Repeat, using 5 drops of iodine solution instead of the chlorine water. *(11) In each case, is there a colour in either layer? (12) If so, in which layer is the colour?*

F. Repeat, testing 3 mL portions of potassium chloride solution separately with bromine water and with iodine solution. Remember to add the 1 mL of TTE. *(13) In each case, is there a colour in either layer? (14) If so, in which layer is the colour?*

G. Finally, test 3 mL portions of potassium iodide solution separately with chlorine water and with bromine water. Remember to add the 1 mL of TTE. *(15) In each case, is there a colour in either layer? (16) If so, in which layer is the colour?*

Concluding Questions

(1) What can you say about the ability of copper atoms to donate electrons to zinc ions? To lead ions?

(2) What can you say about the ability of zinc atoms to donate electrons to copper ions? To lead ions?

(3) What can you say about the ability of lead atoms to donate electrons to copper ions? To zinc ions?

(4) What can you say about the ability of bromide ions to donate electrons to chlorine molecules? To iodine molecules?

(5) What can you say about the ability of chloride ions to donate electrons to bromine molecules? To iodine molecules?

(6) What can you say about the ability of iodide ions to donate electrons to chlorine molecules? To bromine molecules?

(7) What are the equations for the reactions that took place?

(8) Which metal is the strongest reducing agent? The weakest reducing agent?

(9) Which metal ion is the strongest oxidizing agent? The weakest oxidizing agent?

(10) Which halogen is the strongest oxidizing agent? The weakest oxidizing agent?

(11) Which halide ion is the strongest reducing agent? The weakest reducing agent?

(12) Prepare a table with two columns. In the first column arrange the three metals, with the strongest reducing agent at the top and the weakest reducing agent at the bottom. In the other column place the weakest oxidizing agent at the top and the strongest oxidizing agent at the bottom. What do you notice?

(13) Similarly, prepare a table of two columns for the halogens and the halide ions, placing the strongest reducing agent at the upper left, the weakest reducing agent at the lower left, the strongest oxidizing agent at the lower right, and the weakest oxidizing agent at the upper right. What do you notice? Is there any apparent relation between the oxidizing ability of a halogen and its position in the periodic table?

31 Preparation of Hydrogen and the Relative Reactivities of Some Metals

Purpose

(a)   To prepare hydrogen and examine some of its properties.
(b)   To study the relative reactivities of some metals.

Introduction

In this experiment you will produce hydrogen by two different methods, and you will study some of its properties. You will also study the relative abilities of four different metals to produce hydrogen from hydrochloric acid. That is, you will study the relative reactivities of these metals.

Apparatus

25 × 200 mm combustion tube   buret clamp
150 mm test tubes (8)   pneumatic trough
10 mL graduated cylinder   rubber tubing
one-hole rubber stopper   solid rubber stoppers (4)
short glass tube   ring stand

Materials

6 mol/L hydrochloric acid   mossy zinc
6 mol/L sodium hydroxide   aluminum foil
zinc strip   copper wire
magnesium ribbon   iron nail
2 mol/L hydrochloric acid   steel wool

Procedure

A. Set up the apparatus for the collection of hydrogen gas as shown in Fig. 31-1. Make sure the rubber tubing is not pinched and that the gas is free to flow through the tubing into the pneumatic trough. Fill four 150 mm test tubes with water and place them in the trough. CAUTION: Collect the hydrogen only in these 150 mm test tubes. Do not collect larger quantities.

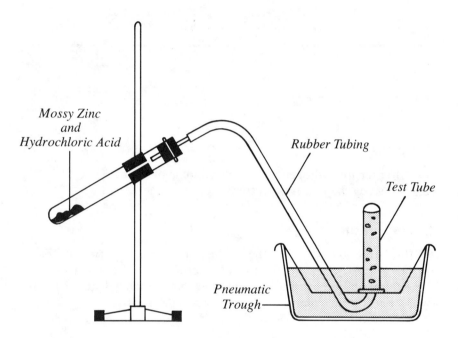

Fig. 31-1 Apparatus for the Preparation of Hydrogen

B. Place about 6 pieces of mossy zinc into the large combustion tube. Add 10 mL of hydrochloric acid to the tube and quickly insert the one-hole stopper as shown in Fig. 31-1. Collect four test tubes of the gas. Stopper the test tubes, and note the order in which they were collected. Put these test tubes of hydrogen aside.

C. Test each test tube of the collected gas in the order in which they were collected by removing the stopper and placing a lighted wooden splint into the mouth of the test tube. *(1) What do you observe in each case? (2) Are all the results the same?*

D. Clean the combustion tube. Fill four 150 mm test tubes with water once again, and place them in the trough. **CAUTION: Collect the hydrogen only in these 150 mm test tubes. Do not collect larger quantities.** Crumple two 4 cm square pieces of aluminum foil, and place them in the combustion tube. Set up the apparatus as shown in Fig. 31-1. Add 10 mL of 6 mol/L sodium hydroxide to the combustion tube and quickly insert the one-hole stopper. Collect four test tubes of hydrogen as in part B.

E. Repeat part C. *(3) What do you observe?*

F. Place 3 mL of 2 mol/L hydrochloric acid into each of four small test tubes. Using steel wool, clean small pieces of copper wire, magnesium ribbon, zinc, and an iron nail. Place each of these in separate test tubes containing the hydrochloric acid. Note the relative reactivity of these metals with hydrochloric acid by observing the relative speed with which hydrogen is produced.

Concluding Questions

(1) What are some physical properties of hydrogen gas?

(2) How would you interpret the results of parts C and E?

(3) Does hydrogen burn? How do you know?

(4) What is the ranking of the four metals in part F in order of their increasing ability to produce hydrogen from hydrochloric acid?

(5) In order for a metal to produce hydrogen from an acid, hydronium ions must receive electrons from the metal to produce $H_2(g)$. Which of the four metals loses electrons most readily? Least readily?

(6) If the products of the reaction in part B are hydrogen gas and aqueous zinc chloride, what is the balanced chemical equation for the reaction?

(7) If the products of the reaction in part D are hydrogen gas and $NaAl(OH)_4(aq)$, what is the balanced chemical equation for the reaction?

(8) What are the balanced chemical equations for the substitution reactions that produce hydrogen in part F?

32 Oxygen — Its Preparation and Properties

Purpose

(a) To prepare oxygen and investigate some of its properties.
(b) To investigate the use of catalysts in the preparation of oxygen.

Introduction

In this experiment, oxygen is prepared by dropping liquid hydrogen peroxide on manganese dioxide powder. The manganese dioxide is used to catalyze the decomposition of hydrogen peroxide so that oxygen gas may be produced much more quickly. No oxygen is evolved from the manganese dioxide. All of the manganese dioxide catalyst can be recovered unchanged at the end of the experiment. You will also examine other catalysts that can aid in the decomposition of hydrogen peroxide to produce oxygen.

Apparatus

burner
250 mL Florence flask
two-hole rubber stopper
bent glass tube (60°)
buret clamp
glass squares (2)
150 mm test tubes (3)

thistle tube
rubber tubing
125 mL wide-mouth bottles (2)
pneumatic trough
ring stand
deflagrating spoon
rubber stopper

Materials

manganese dioxide
6% hydrogen peroxide
3% hydrogen peroxide
charcoal

magnesium ribbon
dry yeast
0.1 mol/L $CuSO_4$
wooden splint

Procedure

A. Set up the apparatus as shown in Fig. 32-1. Spread about 0.5 g (measured by comparison with a display sample) of manganese dioxide on the bottom of a 250 mL Forence flask. Place two water-filled wide-mouth bottles, and one water-filled 150 mm test tube upside down in a trough of water.

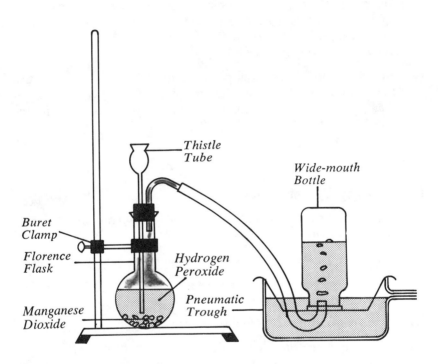

Fig. 32-1 Apparatus for the Preparation and Collection of Oxygen

B. Add 6% hydrogen peroxide to the manganese dioxide to maintain a constant evolution of gas for 15 s, but do not collect this gas. *(1) Why isn't this initial gas collected?* After 15 s begin to collect the gas. Add hydrogen peroxide as needed. Collect two bottles and one test tube of oxygen. After the oxygen has been collected, cover the bottles with glass squares and stopper the test tube. *(2) What can you say about the solubility of oxygen in water?*

C. Light a wooden splint, then blow the flame out so that the splint remains glowing. Quickly thrust the glowing splint into the test tube of oxygen. *(3) What do you observe?*

D. Place some charcoal about the size of a small pea in a deflagrating spoon. Place the spoon in your burner flame until the charcoal begins to glow. Quickly lower the deflagrating spoon into the bottle of oxygen. *(4) What is the result?*

E. Wind the end of a 5 cm strip of magnesium ribbon around the bottom of a deflagrating spoon. Light the other end of the magnesium ribbon in your burner flame. CAUTION: Do not look directly at the burning magnesium; look slightly to one side of it. Quickly lower the burning magnesium into the bottle of oxygen, being careful not to touch the bottle with the magnesium. *(5) What do you observe?*

F. Add 5 mL of 3% hydrogen peroxide to each of two 150 mm test tubes. To one of these tubes add an amount of dry yeast no larger than the head of a match. *(6) What do you observe?* To the second test tube add 2 mL of 0.1 mol/L $CuSO_4$. *(7) What do you observe?*

Concluding Questions

(1) What physical properties of oxygen have you noted during this experiment?

(2) What chemical properties of oxygen have you noted during this experiment?

(3) Does oxygen burn? How do you know?

(4) Does oxygen support combustion? How do you know?

(5) At one time, astronauts in American spacecraft lived and worked in an atmosphere of pure oxygen. This is no longer the case. Why do you suppose the change was made to a different type of atmosphere?

(6) Which appears to be a better catalyst, dry yeast or $CuSO_4$?

33 Purification of Water

Purpose

To study some methods for the purification of water.

Introduction

Filtration and distillation are two methods for purifying water which are often used. Two other common methods are settling and coagulation. If a sediment-laden solution is allowed to stand undisturbed, the solid particles will slowly settle to the bottom of the container. Alternatively, it is possible to add to the water a chemical that causes a precipitate to form. The newly formed precipitate carries suspended solids with it as it settles fairly rapidly to the bottom of the container. In this experiment you will evaluate the effectiveness of the four methods in removing various types of impurity from water.

Apparatus

10 mL graduated cylinder
50 mL graduated cylinder
200 mm test tubes (4)
150 mL beakers (4)
stirring rod
spatula
filter paper
funnel
iron ring
ring stands (2)
burner

wire gauze
250 mL Florence flask
buret clamp
condenser clamp
two-hole rubber stopper
    for Florence flask
thermometer
bent glass tube
one-hole rubber stopper for condenser
condenser
rubber tubing (2)

Materials

0.01 mol/L aluminum sulfate
0.01 mol/L calcium hydroxide
muddy water

potassium permanganate
barium sulfate
boiling chips

Procedure

A. In a 200 mm test tube, place 16 mL of calcium hydroxide solution. Slowly add 4 mL of aluminum sulfate solution. *(1) What do you observe?*

B. In each of three 200 mm test tubes labelled A, B, and C, place 10 mL of muddy water. To tube A add 10 mL of tap water and mix well. To tube B add 8 mL of calcium hydroxide solution and 2 mL of aluminum sulfate solution and mix well. To tube C add 5 mL of tap water, 4 mL of calcium hydroxide solution, and 1 mL of aluminum sulfate solution and mix well. Observe each mixture as it is prepared and every 5 min for the next 20 to 25 min. *(2) What do you observe in each tube when each mixture is initially prepared? (3) What do you observe in each tube as time passes?* Proceed to part C while you continue to make these observations every 5 min.

C. To 100 mL of water in a 150 mL beaker, add a few small grains of potassium permanganate and stir. *(4) What do you observe?* Retain this mixture for parts E and F.

D. To 100 mL of water in a 150 mL beaker, add a spatula full of barium sulfate and stir. *(5) What do you observe?* Retain this mixture for parts E and F.

E. Filter a portion (about 10 mL) of the potassium permanganate-water mixture. *(6) What do you observe?* Filter a portion (about 10 mL) of the barium sulfate-water mixture. *(7) What do you observe?*

F. Set up a distillation apparatus as instructed by your teacher (or as in Fig. 33-1). Pour into the Florence flask the mixture from part E that was least affected by filtration. Add a boiling chip, heat to boiling, and collect a few millilitres of distillate. *(8) What do you observe?*

Concluding Questions

(1) What is the balanced equation for the reaction in part A?

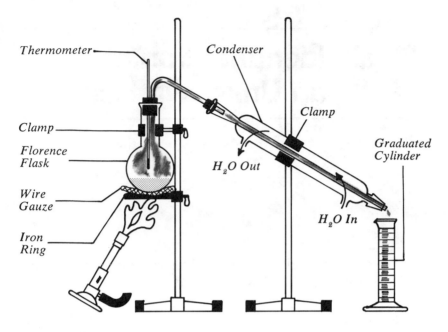

Fig. 33-1 Distillation Apparatus

(2) On the basis of your observations in part B, would you say that coagulation using calcium hydroxide and aluminum sulfate is a more efficient or a less efficient method of removing suspended solids from water than is settling?

(3) Is the purification process more efficient when small amounts or large amounts of precipitating chemicals are added?

(4) Is potassium permanganate soluble in water? How do you know?

(5) Is barium sulfate soluble in water? How do you know?

(6) Does filtration remove from water a substance that is soluble in it? How do you know?

(7) How do you explain any differences in the effectiveness of filtration in removing these two types (soluble or insoluble) of impurity?

(8) Was distillation effective in removing the impurity from the mixture in Part F?

(9) For what type of mixture should distillation rather than filtration be used as a method of separation? Explain your answer.

34 Identification of an Unknown Halide

Purpose

To determine the similarities and differences in the properties of the halide ions, and to use these differences to identify an unknown halide.

Introduction

The properties of the elements vary in a regular manner from left to right and from top to bottom of the periodic table. Thus, from your knowledge of the periodic table, you would expect the properties of the halogens or of the halide ions to be similar but not identical, because the elements are all in Group VII.

In this experiment you will determine some of the similarities and differences in the properties of the halide ions. You will then use these differences to devise a scheme which will enable you to identify the halide ion in an unknown solution.

Apparatus

150 mm test tubes (9)   cork stoppers
medicine droppers

Materials

0.1 mol/L sodium chloride   6 mol/L nitric acid
0.1 mol/L sodium bromide   3% hydrogen peroxide
0.1 mol/L sodium iodide   0.02 mol/L potassium
0.1 mol/L silver nitrate   permanganate
6 mol/L ammonia   trichlorotrifluoroethane (TTE)
0.1 mol/L sodium thiosulfate

Procedure

A. Prepare a data table as shown. Record all experimental results in the data table as soon as you obtain them. Complete the remainder of the data table as soon as you have enough data to do so.

Data Table 34-1

Reagent	Observations		
	Chloride	Bromide	Iodide
$AgNO_3$ $AgNO_3 + NH_3$ $AgNO_3$ and NH_3 $+ Na_2S_2O_3$ H_2O_2 and HNO_3 $KMnO_4$ and HNO_3			

B. In a clean test tube, place 10 drops of sodium chloride solution. In a second test tube place 10 drops of sodium bromide solution. In a third test tube place 10 drops of sodium iodide solution. To each test tube add 5 drops of silver nitrate solution. Next, add 10 drops of aqueous ammonia to each test tube. Finally, to each test tube which still contains a precipitate, add 10 drops of sodium thiosulfate solution.

C. In each of two clean, labelled test tubes place 10 drops of sodium chloride solution. In the same way prepare two test tubes of sodium bromide solution and two test tubes of sodium iodide solution. To each of the six test tubes add 5 drops of dilute nitric acid and 10 drops of TTE. To one of the test tubes containing sodium chloride, add 15 drops of hydrogen peroxide solution, stopper it with a cork, and shake vigorously. Repeat with one of the test tubes containing sodium bromide and one of the tubes containing sodium iodide. To each of the remaining test tubes add 10 drops of potassium permanganate solution, stopper, and shake well.

D. Use the results of your observations to devise a means of determining whether an unknown solution contains chloride, bromide, or iodide ions. Check your method with your teacher. Then obtain an unknown from your teacher and identify it.

Concluding Questions

(1) Why is TTE used to note the reactions in part C?

(2) What is the reasoning which you used to identify your unknown?

(3) Which halide ion was present in your unknown?

(4) What is an important practical use of the reaction with sodium thiosulfate?

35 Analysis of a Chemical Reaction

Purpose

To observe a chemical reaction and to use qualitative and quantitative evidence to identify this reaction from among four possibilities.

Introduction

In this experiment you will heat a common household chemical, baking soda (sodium hydrogen carbonate), which has the chemical formula $NaHCO_3$. The reaction which occurs is one of the following:

$$NaHCO_3(s) \xrightarrow{\Delta} NaOH(s) + CO_2(g)$$
$$2NaHCO_3(s) \xrightarrow{\Delta} Na_2CO_3(s) + CO_2(g) + H_2O(g)$$
$$2NaHCO_3(s) \xrightarrow{\Delta} Na_2O(s) + 2CO_2(g) + H_2O(g)$$
$$4NaHCO_3(s) \xrightarrow{\Delta} 2Na_2C_2O_4(s) + O_2(g) + 2H_2O(g)$$

You will choose the correct equation for this reaction based on qualitative observations (observations that are not based on measurements) and quantitative observations (observations that are based on measurements).

Apparatus

150 mm test tubes (2)	clay triangle
buret clamp	iron ring
burner	crucible and cover
ring stand	wire gauze

Materials

sodium hydrogen carbonate   limewater

Procedure

A. Add about 0.5 g of NaHCO$_3$ (compared with a sample on display) to a test tube. Obtain a test tube half-filled with limewater. Set up the apparatus as shown in Fig. 35-1 with the NaHCO$_3$ spread out in the test tube. Heat the NaHCO$_3$ gently for 2 min while holding the test tube of limewater as indicated in Fig. 35-1. After 2 min shake the test tube containing limewater. *(1) What do you observe? (2) What does this result indicate? (3) What do you observe in the test tube that you heated? (4) What does this indicate? (5) Based on these two qualitative observations which of the four possible reactions can be ruled out? Why?*

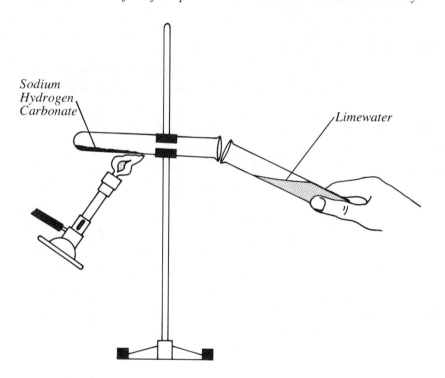

Sodium Hydrogen Carbonate

Limewater

Fig. 35-1 Heating NaHCO$_3$ for Qualitative Test

B. To determine which of the remaining possible reactions is the correct one you must obtain quantitative evidence. Prepare a data table as shown. Record all experimental results in the data table as soon as you obtain them. Complete the remainder of the data table as soon as you have enough data to do so.

Data Table 35-1

Mass of crucible and cover	———————	g
Mass of crucible, cover, and $NaHCO_3$	———————	g
Mass of $NaHCO_3$	———————	g
Mass of crucible, cover, and residue (after heating)	———————	g
Mass of residue	———————	g
Ratio: $\dfrac{\text{Mass of } NaHCO_3}{\text{Mass of residue}}$	———————	

C. Determine the mass of a clean, dry crucible and cover. Add about 1.5 g of $NaHCO_3$ to the crucible and determine the mass of the crucible, cover, and $NaHCO_3$.

D. Place the crucible, with its cover slightly ajar, on a triangle placed on a ring stand. Heat gently for 1 min and then heat strongly for 6 min. Place the crucible and cover on a wire gauze and allow them to cool. Then determine the mass of the crucible, cover, and residue.

E. For each of the remaining possible equations representing the heating of $NaHCO_3$, calculate the ratio of the mass of $NaHCO_3$ to the mass of solid product after heating. *(6) What are the values of these ratios? (7) Which of these ratios agrees with the experimentally determined ratio?*

Concluding Questions

(1) What is the chemical equation that correctly represents the heating of $NaHCO_3$?

(2) What is the evidence for choosing this equation?

(3) What is the percentage error in the experimentally determined ratio (compared with the predicted theoretical ratio)?

36 The Formula of a Hydrate

Purpose

To determine the formula of an unknown hydrate.

Introduction

When water is evaporated from an aqueous solution of a salt, water molecules often become incorporated into the crystals of salt that form. These crystals may appear to be dry, but they will yield a quantity of water when heated. Salts which contain water as part of their crystal structure are called *hydrates* and the water is called *water of hydration*.

In this experiment you will be given an unknown hydrate. Your teacher will provide you with a list of possible formulas for your hydrate. When the hydrate is heated, water is given off:

$$M_aX_b \cdot xH_2O(s) \xrightarrow{\Delta} M_aX_b(s) + xH_2O(g)$$

You can determine the mass of water lost when a known mass of a hydrate is heated, and use this information to calculate the percentage of water by mass in the hydrate. You can compare this value to the percentages of water in the hydrates on the list. Then you can identify your unknown hydrate.

Apparatus

crucible and cover	ring stand	wire gauze
clay triangle	burner	crucible tongs
iron ring		

Materials

unknown hydrate

Procedure

A. Prepare a data table as shown. Record all experimental results in the data table as soon as you obtain them. Complete the remainder of the data table as soon as you have enough data to do so.

Data Table 36-1

Mass of crucible and cover	_____ g
Mass of crucible, cover, and hydrate	_____ g
Mass of hydrate	_____ g
Mass of crucible, cover, and dehydrated solid (first heating)	_____ g
Mass of crucible, cover, and dehydrated solid (second heating)	_____ g
Mass of water lost	_____ g
Percentage by mass of water in the hydrate	_____ %
Formula of the unknown hydrate	_____

B. Place a clean, dry crucible and cover on a triangle placed on a ring stand. The crucible cover should be slightly ajar. Heat the crucible strongly with a burner for 3 min, then place the crucible and cover on a wire gauze to cool for 5 min. Determine the mass of the crucible and cover.

C. Place about 4 g of the unknown hydrate in the crucible. Determine the mass of the crucible, cover, and hydrate.

D. Place the crucible, with its cover slightly ajar, on the triangle. Heat very gently for 5 min or until hissing or sizzling has stopped. Avoid spattering the contents of the crucible. Increase the flame until the crucible bottom is a dull red, and heat for 5 min. Place the crucible and cover on a wire gauze to cool for 5 min, then determine the mass of the crucible, cover, and contents.

E. Reheat the crucible, cover, and contents to dull redness for 3 min, cool, and redetermine the mass of the crucible, cover, and contents. Your measurements from parts D and E should agree within 0.03 g. If they do not agree, repeat part E.

Concluding Questions

(1) What is the purpose of the initial heating and cooling in part B?

(2) What is the purpose of the second heating and cooling in part E?

(3) If your unknown had contained some crystals that had already lost their water of hydration, how would the results of the experiment have been affected?

37 Mass Relationships in a Chemical Reaction

Purpose

To determine the mass of copper formed when excess aluminum is allowed to react with a given mass of a copper salt.

Introduction

In this experiment, a piece of aluminum foil will be placed in an aqueous solution of copper(II) chloride. The reaction is allowed to go to completion. The mass of copper produced when 2.00 g of the copper compound react with excess aluminum will be determined.

Apparatus

150 mL beaker	iron ring
stirring rod	wire gauze
ruler	tweezers
burner	50 mL graduated cylinder
ring stand	watch glass

Materials

$CuCl_2 \cdot 2H_2O$ aluminum foil

Procedure

A.   Prepare a data table as shown. Record all experimental results in the data table as soon as you obtain them. Complete the remainder of the data table as soon as you have enough data to do so.

Data Table 37-1

Mass of beaker	————————g
Mass of beaker $+ CuCl_2 \cdot 2H_2O$	————————g
Mass of $CuCl_2 \cdot 2H_2O$	————————g
Mass of beaker $+ Cu$	————————g
Mass of Cu	————————g

B. Determine the mass of a clean, dry 150 mL beaker. To the beaker add 2.00 g of copper(II) chloride dihydrate. Determine the mass of the beaker and contents. Add 50 mL of water. Stir to dissolve the copper compound.

C. Fold a 6 cm × 10 cm piece of aluminum foil lengthwise to make a 3 cm × 10 cm strip. Then fold this lengthwise again to make a 1.5 cm × 10 cm strip. Loosely coil the strip into a circle, and place it in the solution so that it lies on its edge on the bottom of the beaker.

D. Place the beaker on a wire gauze on a ring stand, and heat the solution with a burner until it has boiled *gently* for 5 min. Avoid overheating. There may be some foaming during the early stages of the heating. Allow the solution to cool until you can hold it comfortably in your hands.

E. Carefully use tweezers to shake any remaining aluminum foil in the beaker to dislodge the copper. Remove the aluminum foil, being careful to leave the copper in the beaker. Pour the liquid in the beaker into the sink, being careful not to lose any copper. Add 50 mL of water to the beaker. Stir well to wash the copper, and discard the water into the sink, being careful not to lose any copper. Repeat the washing with another 50 mL of water, again being careful not to lose any copper.

F. Cover the beaker with a watch glass, and *gently* heat the beaker containing the wet copper to drive off the water. When the initial spattering has stopped, remove the watch glass and continue the gentle heating to drive off the last traces of moisture. Do not heat so strongly that the copper begins to turn black.

G. Allow the beaker to cool, and determine the mass of the beaker and copper.

Concluding Questions

(1) How many grams of Cu should be produced when 2.00 g of $CuCl_2 \cdot 2H_2O$ reacts with excess Al according to the following equation?

$$3CuCl_2 \cdot 2H_2O + 2Al \rightarrow 3Cu + 2AlCl_3 + 6H_2O$$

(2) What is the difference between the theoretical mass of Cu (from question 1) and the actual mass determined in the experiment? Subtract the smaller number from the larger number.

(3) What is the percentage error according to the equation

$$\% \text{ Error} = \frac{\text{difference between theoretical and actual masses}}{\text{theoretical mass}} \times 100$$

(4) How many grams of Al would be required to react with 2.00 g of $CuCl_2 \cdot 2H_2O$?

(5) How many grams of $AlCl_3$ would be formed if 3.00 g of Al were allowed to react with 3.00 g of $CuCl_2 \cdot 2H_2O$?

38 Standardization of a Basic Solution by Titration

Purpose

To standardize a sodium hydroxide solution by acid-base titration.

Introduction

In this experiment you will determine the concentration of (that is, standardize) a sodium hydroxide solution by acid-base titration. Titration is the name given to the technique of carefully measuring the volume of a solution required to react with a known amount of another reagent.

A known quantity of a solid acid (potassium hydrogen phthalate) is dissolved in water in a flask, and phenophthalein indicator is added. The sodium hydroxide solution is titrated from a buret into the flask containing the acid. The acid and the base react with one another according to the equation

$$KHC_8H_4O_4 \text{ (aq) } + NaOH(aq) \rightarrow KNaC_8H_4O_4(aq) + H_2O(\ell)$$

During the first stages of the titration, the sodium hydroxide will be completely neutralized, and an excess of acid will remain. However, eventually there will be a point at which the sodium hydroxide is neutralized by the last portion of acid. At this point, the theoretical endpoint, the acid and the base have neutralized one another exactly, and no more base should be added to the flask. The endpoint volume of base, measured with the buret, is used to determine the concentration of the basic solution.

The phenolphthalein indicator is used to determine experimentally the point at which the base has neutralized all of the acid. This is called the experimental endpoint. Phenolphthalein is colourless in acid solution. It turns pink when the acid is completely neutralized and a slight excess of base is present. Thus, this experimental endpoint differs slightly from the theoretical endpoint because the former cannot be detected unless there is a slight excess of base. In this titration, a successful endpoint is achieved if one drop of base from the buret turns the solution in the flask from colourless to pink. When that happens, you know that the experimental endpoint differs from the theoretical endpoint by less than one drop of the basic solution.

Since you know the mass of potassium hydrogen phthalate ($KHC_8H_4O_4$), you can calculate the numbers of moles of acid. At this endpoint, the number of moles of acid equals the number of moles of base. Thus, you know the number of moles of base in the endpoint volume of base, and you can calculate the concentration of the sodium hydroxide solution using the equation

$$x \text{ mol/L} = \frac{y \text{ mol}}{z \text{ L}}$$

Although potassium hydrogen phthalate is often used as the solid acid for the standardization of a basic solution by titration, other solid acids can be used, including potassium hydrogen oxalate and potassium hydrogen sulfate. You will be told if an alternative solid acid is to be used.

The apparatus used to measure the sodium hydroxide solution is called a buret. A buret is a graduated glass tube with a valve at the bottom. Three types of valves which can be used to regulate the flow of the sodium hydroxide solution through the buret tip are shown in Fig. 38-1. If the buret has a glass bead in a piece of rubber tubing, you can control the rate of flow by exerting gentle pressure on the portion of the tubing that covers the glass bead. If the buret has a pinch clamp on rubber tubing, you can control the rate of flow by releasing the pinch clamp slightly. If the buret has a stopcock, you can control the rate of flow by rotating the stopcock slowly until the solution starts to come out of the buret tip. Stopcocks can be made of glass or of Teflon®.

If a buret with a glass stopcock is used to contain a basic solution, extra care must be taken. A basic solution tends to cement a glass stopcock so firmly that it is difficult to remove. Thus, if basic solutions are titrated from burets with glass stopcocks, the stopcock must be removed from the buret at the end of the laboratory period, and both buret and stopcock must be rinsed thoroughly with distilled water to remove *all* traces of the base. In many laboratories, burets with glass stopcocks are never used for basic solutions.

A liquid placed in a buret forms a curved meniscus at its upper surface. In the case of water or aqueous solutions, the meniscus is concave, and buret readings are obtained by determining the position of the bottom of the meniscus. Furthermore, the eye must be on a level with the meniscus, as shown in Fig. 5-1. Remember that a buret is read

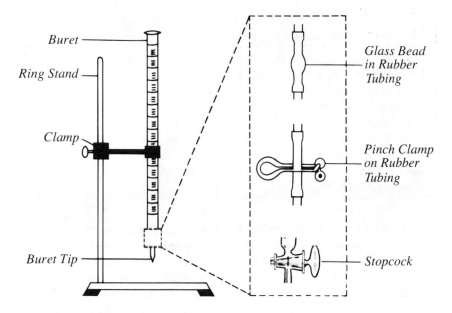

Fig. 38-1 The Buret

from top to bottom and not from bottom to top. That is, the 0 mL mark is near the top of the buret and the 50 mL mark is near the bottom.

Apparatus

150 mL beaker
50 mL buret
buret clamp
ring stand

250 mL Erlenmeyer flasks (2)
50 mL graduated cylinder
250 mL beaker

Materials

sodium hydroxide solution
phenolphthalein solution

potassium hydrogen phthalate

Procedure

A. Prepare a data table as shown. Record all experimental results in the data table as soon as you obtain them. Complete the remainder of the data table as soon as you have enough data to do so.

Data Table 38-1

Measurements and Results	#1	#2
Initial mass of vial and acid	——— g	——— g
Final mass of vial and acid	——— g	——— g
Mass of acid used	——— g	——— g
Final reading of buret	——— mL	——— mL
Initial reading of buret	——— mL	——— mL
Volume of NaOH used	——— mL	——— mL
Moles of acid used	——— mol	——— mol
Moles of NaOH used	——— mol	——— mol
Concentration of NaOH	——— mol/L	——— mol/L

B. Label two Erlenmeyer flasks 1 and 2. Place about 2.5 g of potassium hydrogen phthalate (measured by comparison with a display sample) in a vial. Determine the mass of the vial and contents. Pour about one-half of the solid acid into the first flask. Determine the mass of the vial and contents a second time. Between 1.00 g and 1.50 g of solid acid should now be in the first flask. Pour the rest of the solid acid into the second flask. Determine the mass of the vial a third time. Notice that the second mass determination appears in the data table twice. It is the final mass of vial and acid in column 1, and it is also the initial mass of vial and acid in column 2. Dissolve each sample in 50 mL of distilled water.

C. Obtain about 120 mL of sodium hydroxide solution in a 150 mL beaker. Rinse the buret with about 10 mL of this solution, and let the liquid drain through the buret tip into an empty 250 mL beaker. Repeat this procedure twice more. Refill the buret so that the meniscus is above the zero mark, and fasten it to a ring stand with a buret clamp. Let some of the sodium hydroxide solution run rapidly from the buret to expel all air bubbles from the tip and to bring the level of the solution down to the calibrated region of the buret. If there is a drop of solution hanging on the buret tip, remove it by touching the drop to the inside wall of the 250 mL beaker. Hold a piece of white paper behind the meniscus, and read the initial volume of the sodium hydroxide solution.

D. Add 2 drops of phenolphthalein indicator to each of the Erlenmeyer flasks, and swirl the flask to ensure mixing.

E. Place one of the Erlenmeyer flasks under the tip of the buret. A piece of white paper placed under the flask will make it easier to see the colour changes. While continuously swirling the flask to ensure thorough mixing, run in the sodium hydroxide solution from the buret. Initially, a pink colour appears, and then disappears quickly, at the point where the sodium hydroxide solution comes in contact with the solution in the flask. As the endpoint is approached, the colour disappears more slowly. From this point on, the sodium hydroxide solution should be added drop by drop until one drop turns the entire solution in the flask pink. The pink colour should remain at least 15 s while the solution is being swirled. This colour change indicates that enough sodium hydroxide solution has been added to neutralize all of the acid. Read the final volume of the sodium hydroxide solution.

F. Refill the buret and repeat the titration using the second flask.

Concluding Questions

(1) Why must the buret be rinsed with sodium hydroxide solution before it is filled?

(2) Why must the air bubbles be expelled from the buret tip?

(3) Why does a pink colour appear, and then disappear, at the point where the sodium hydroxide solution comes in contact with the solution in the flask?

(4) What is the concentration of a NaOH solution if 32.47 mL of it are required to neutralize 1.27 g of $KHC_8H_4O_4$?

(5) What is the percentage of $KHC_8H_4O_4$ in a sample if 2.81 g of the sample requires 35.61 mL of 0.152 mol/L NaOH to neutralize it?

39 Acid-Base Titration

Purpose

To standardize a solution of hydrochloric acid by acid-base titration.

Introduction

In this experiment, you will titrate a known volume of hydrochloric acid with a solution of sodium hydroxide of known concentration. The acid and the base react with one another according to the equation

$$HCl(aq) + NaOH(aq) \rightarrow NaCl(aq) + H_2O(\ell)$$

The hydrochloric acid is placed in an Erlenmeyer flask, and phenolphthalein indicator is added. The sodium hydroxide solution is titrated from a buret into the flask containing the acid. During the first stages of the titration, the sodium hydroxide will be completely neutralized, and an excess of acid will remain. However, eventually there will be a point, the theoretical endpoint, at which the acid and the base have neutralized one another exactly, and no more base should be added to the flask.

The phenolphthalein indicator is used to determine experimentally the point, called the experimental endpoint, at which the base has neutralized the acid. Phenophthalein is colourless in acid solution. It turns pink when the acid is completely neutralized and a slight excess of base is present. Because this experimental endpoint cannot be detected unless there is a slight excess of base, it differs slightly from the theoretical endpoint. In this titration, a successful endpoint is achieved if one drop of base turns the solution in the flask from colourless to pink. When this happens, the experimental endpoint differs from the theoretical endpoint by less than one drop of base.

In this experiment, you will use separate burets for the acid and the base. It is advantageous to use two burets. If you should overshoot the endpoint by adding too much base, you will be able to add an additional measured volume of acid from the acid buret. The additional acid will neutralize the excess base, and you can then add more base to reach a new endpoint. Burets are described in the introduction to Experiment 38. Notice that extra care must be taken if a buret with a glass stopcock is used to contain a basic solution.

At the endpoint, the number of moles of hydrochloric acid used equals the number of moles of sodium hydroxide used. Since you know both the concentration in moles per litre and the volume in millilitres (which you can convert to litres) of the sodium hydroxide, you can calculate the number of moles of base used. Thus, you know the number of moles of hydrochloric acid in the measured volume of acid, and you can calculate the concentration of the hydrochloric acid using the equation

$$x \text{ mol/L} = \frac{y \text{ mol}}{z \text{ L}}$$

Apparatus

150 mL beakers (2)   ring stand
50 mL burets (2)   250 mL Erlenmeyer flasks (3)
double buret clamp   250 mL beakers (2)

Materials

standardized NaOH solution   unknown HCl solution
phenolphthalein solution

Procedure

A. Prepare a data table as shown. Record all experimental results in the data table as soon as you obtain them. Complete the remainder of the data table as soon as you have enough data to do so.

Data Table 39-1

Measurements and Results	#1	#2	#3
Concentration of NaOH	_____ mol/L	_____ mol/L	_____ mol/L
Final reading of base buret	_____ mL	_____ mL	_____ mL
Initial reading of base buret	_____ mL	_____ mL	_____ mL
Volume of NaOH used	_____ mL	_____ mL	_____ mL
Final reading of acid buret	_____ mL	_____ mL	_____ mL
Initial reading of acid buret	_____ mL	_____ mL	_____ mL
Volume of HCl used	_____ mL	_____ mL	_____ mL
Moles of NaOH used	_____ mol	_____ mol	_____ mol
Moles of HCl used	_____ mol	_____ mol	_____ mol
Concentration of HCl	_____ mol/L	_____ mol/L	_____ mol/L

B. Obtain about 120 mL of hydrochloric acid solution in a 150 mL beaker. Label the beaker. Rinse a buret with about 10 mL of the solution, and let the liquid drain through the buret tip into an empty 250 mL beaker. Repeat this procedure twice more. Refill the buret so that the meniscus of the solution is above the zero mark. Position the buret in a double buret clamp on a ring stand, as shown in Fig. 39-1. Let some of the solution run rapidly from the buret to expel all air bubbles from the tip and to bring the level of the solution down to the calibrated region of the buret. If there is a drop of solution hanging on the buret tip, remove it by touching the drop to the inside wall of the 250 mL beaker. Hold a piece of white paper behind the meniscus, and read the initial volume of the solution at the bottom of the meniscus. Your eye must be at the same level as the meniscus, as shown in Fig. 5-1.

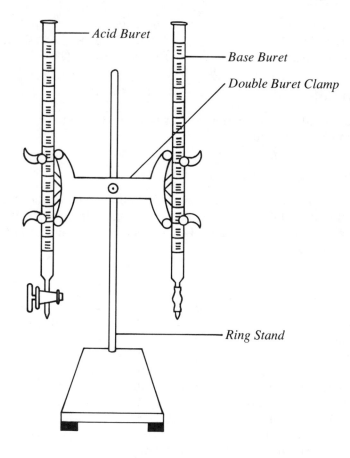

Fig. 39-1 Two Burets for Acid-Base Titrations

C. Obtain about 120 mL of sodium hydroxide in a second labelled 150 mL beaker. Obtain a second buret and repeat part B.

D. Let about 20 mL of hydrochloric acid flow from the acid buret into a clean 250 mL Erlenmeyer flask. Add 2 drops of phenolphthalein. Place the Erlenmeyer flask under the tip of the base buret. A piece of white paper placed under the flask will make it easier to see the colour changes. While continuously swirling the flask to ensure thorough mixing, run in the sodium hydroxide solution from the buret. Initially a pink colour appears, and then disappears quickly, at the point where the sodium hydroxide solution comes in contact with the solution in the flask. As the endpoint is approached, the colour disappears more slowly. From this point on, the sodium hydroxide solution should be added drop by drop until one drop turns the entire solution in the flask pink. This pink colour should remain at least 15 s while the solution is being swirled. If you overshoot the endpoint, add more acid from the acid buret until the solution becomes colourless again. Then add the sodium hydroxide from the base buret until you have the faint pink endpoint. When you have a satisfactory endpoint, read the final volume of each buret.

E. Refill each buret and repeat part D twice more.

Concluding Questions

(1) Why does the pink colour which forms at the point where the sodium hydroxide comes in contact with the solution in the flask disappear more slowly near the endpoint?

(2) Why is it a good idea to carry out titrations in triplicate?

(3) What is the average value of the concentration of the hydrochloric acid?

(4) If 27.31 mL of 0.211 mol/L NaOH is able to neutralize 37.45 mL of HCl, what is the concentration of the HCl?

(5) What volume of 0.117 mol/L HCl is needed to neutralize 28.67 mL of 0.137 mol/L KOH?

(6) If 35.93 mL of 0.159 mol/L NaOH is able to neutralize 27.48 mL of H_2SO_4 according to the equation

$$H_2SO_4 \text{ (aq)} + 2NaOH(aq) \rightarrow Na_2SO_4 + 2H_2O(\ell)$$

what is the concentration of the H_2SO_4?

40 The Effect of Pressure on the Volume of a Gas

Purpose

To discover the relationship between the volume of a given quantity of a gas and the pressure exerted on the gas.

Introduction

In this experiment a fixed quantity of a gas (air) is trapped in a syringe. Most syringes measure volume in cubic centimetres and the manufacturers use the abbreviation c.c., rather than the SI symbol cm^3. However, since the volumes of gases are usually measured in litres or millilitres, we will measure the volume of the gas trapped in the syringe in millilitres rather than cubic centimetres.

The pressure exerted by the trapped gas is equal to the pressure exerted on it by the atmosphere plus the additional pressure caused by the piston and platform assembly (Fig. 40-1). We live at the bottom of an ''ocean'' of air, and the atmospheric pressure exerted on the trapped gas is a result of the mass of the column of air that rests on the piston. Furthermore, the mass of the piston, platform, and any other object(s) placed on the platform cause an additional pressure to be exerted on the trapped gas.

We can relate pressure and mass mathematically. Pressure is caused by a force F distributed over an area A:

$$P = \frac{F}{A} \tag{1}$$

Force is the product of mass m times acceleration a:

$$F = m\,a \tag{2}$$

Substitution of equation (2) in equation (1) gives

$$P = \frac{m\,a}{A} \qquad (3)$$

In this experiment the acceleration is the acceleration due to gravity, which is constant, and the area is the area of the piston (πr^2), which is also constant. The only variables are pressure and mass, and equation (3) can be simplified, becoming

$$P = k\,m$$

For example, if the total mass of the piston, platform, and an object placed on the platform were 1.00 kg, and the acceleration due to gravity were 9.81 m/s², the force would be

$$F = m\,a = 1.00 \text{ kg} \times 9.81 \text{ m/s}^2$$
$$= 9.81 \text{ kg} \cdot \text{m/s}^2$$
$$= 9.81 \text{ N}$$

If the diameter of the piston were 2.66 cm (0.0266 m), the area would be

$$A = \pi r^2 = 3.14 \times (0.0133 \text{ m})^2$$
$$= 5.56 \times 10^{-4}\,\text{m}^2$$

The pressure created by the 1.00 kg on the trapped gas would be

$$P = \frac{F}{A} = \frac{9.81 \text{ N}}{5.56 \times 10^{-4}\,\text{m}^2}$$
$$= 17\,600 \text{ N/m}^2$$
$$= 17\,600 \text{ Pa}$$
$$= 17.6 \text{ kPa}$$

Thus, in this example the pressure caused by the mass of the piston, platform, and object(s) on the platform would be

$$P = 17.6 \text{ kPa/kg} \times m$$

where m is the total mass (in kilograms) of the piston, platform, and object(s) on the platform.

Your teacher will provide the information necessary for you to determine the pressure caused by the mass of the piston, platform, and object(s) on the platform. This pressure plus the atmospheric pressure equals the total pressure exerted on the trapped gas. You will increase the pressure exerted on the trapped gas by placing more objects on the platform.

Apparatus

60 mL syringe (with platform)   buret clamp
rubber stopper   objects (e.g. books)
ring stand

Procedure

A. Prepare a data table as shown. Record all experimental results as soon as you obtain them. Complete the remainder of the data table as soon as you have enough data to do so.

Data Table 40-1

Atmospheric pressure				_____ kPa		
Pressure per kilogram caused by total mass				_____ kPa/kg		
Mass of piston and platform assembly				_____ kg		

Number of Objects	Mass of Added Object	Total Mass	Total Pressure (P)	Total Volume (V)	P V Product
0	0	_____ kg	_____ kPa	_____ mL	_____
1	_____ kg	_____ kg	_____ kPa	_____ mL	_____
2	_____ kg	_____ kg	_____ kPa	_____ mL	_____
3	_____ kg	_____ kg	_____ kPa	_____ mL	_____
4	_____ kg	_____ kg	_____ kPa	_____ mL	_____
5	_____ kg	_____ kg	_____ kPa	_____ mL	_____
6	_____ kg	_____ kg	_____ kPa	_____ mL	_____

B. Determine the mass of the piston and platform assembly.

C. Lubricate the piston with a drop of glycerol. Adjust the piston and platform assembly in the syringe so that the volume is about 55 mL. Place the tip of the syringe in a small hole which has been drilled into, but not through, a rubber stopper. The syringe must fit tightly into the hole so that none of the trapped gas will escape. Clamp the syringe firmly to a ring stand, as shown in Fig. 40-1.

D. Push the piston into the syringe, and release it, several times. Then read the volume of the trapped gas. The total pressure exerted on the trapped gas is the atmospheric pressure plus a small additional pressure caused by the mass of the piston and platform assembly.

E. Determine the mass of an object such as a book. Carefully balance the object on the platform. Push the piston into the syringe, and release it, several times. Then read the volume of the

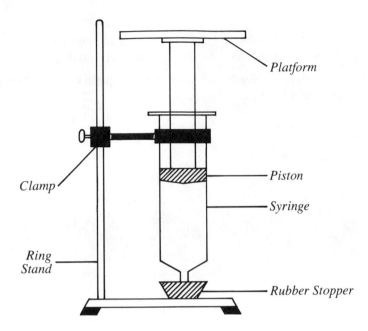

Fig. 40-1 Piston and Platform Assembly

trapped gas. The total pressure exerted on the trapped gas is the atmospheric pressure plus an additional pressure caused by the total mass of the piston, platform, and object(s) on the platform.

F. Repeat part E using additional objects carefully balanced on the platform. In each case, the total pressure exerted on the trapped gas is the atmospheric pressure plus an additional pressure caused by the total mass of the piston, platform, and objects on the platform. It is unlikely that the piston of a 60 mL syringe can hold much more than 7 kg.

Concluding Questions

(1) What is the effect of an increase of pressure on the volume of the trapped gas?

(2) What can you say about the constancy of the PV products?

(3) What type of graph is obtained if volume (vertical axis) is plotted against pressure (horizontal axis)?

(4) What type of graph is obtained if volume (vertical axis) is plotted against 1/pressure (i.e., the reciprocal of pressure)?

(5) What is the relationship between the pressure and the volume of a given quantity of a gas at a constant temperature?

(6) If the pressure exerted on your trapped gas had been 130 kPa, what would have been its volume?

41 The Effect of Temperature on the Volume of a Gas

Purpose

To discover the relationship between the volume and the temperature of a given quantity of a gas.

Introduction

In this experiment a fixed quantity of a gas (air) is trapped in a syringe. Most syringes measure volume in cubic centimetres, and manufacturers use the abbreviation c.c. rather than the SI symbol cm^3. However, since the volumes of gases are usually measured in litres or millilitres, we will measure the volume of the gas trapped in the syringe in millilitres rather than cubic centimetres.

The temperature of the trapped gas can be varied by immersing the syringe in a beaker of water, the temperature of which can be adjusted to any desired value. We will use two temperature scales — Celsius and Kelvin. The Kelvin temperature is obtained by adding 273° to the Celsius temperature.

Apparatus

30 mL syringe	thermometer	buret clamp
400 mL beaker	iron ring	burner
rubber stopper	ring stand	stirring rod
wire gauze		

Procedure

A. Prepare a data table as shown. Record all experimental results in the data table as soon as you obtain them. Complete the remainder of the data table as soon as you have enough data to do so.

131

Data Table 41-1

Temperature *(t)*	Temperature *(T)*	Volume	*V/t* ratio	*V/T* ratio
———— °C	———— K	———— mL	————	————
———— °C	———— K	———— mL	————	————
———— °C	———— K	———— mL	————	————
———— °C	———— K	———— mL	————	————
———— °C	———— K	———— mL	————	————
———— °C	———— K	———— mL	————	————
———— °C	———— K	———— mL	————	————
———— °C	———— K	———— mL	————	————

B. Lubricate the piston with a drop of glycerol. Adjust the piston in the syringe so that the volume is about 15 mL. Place the tip of the syringe in a small hole which has been drilled into, but not through, a rubber stopper. The syringe must fit tightly into the hole so that none of the trapped gas will escape. Place a beaker of cold tap water on a wire gauze supported by a ring stand. Clamp the syringe to the ring stand so that it is immersed in the cold water (Fig. 41-1).

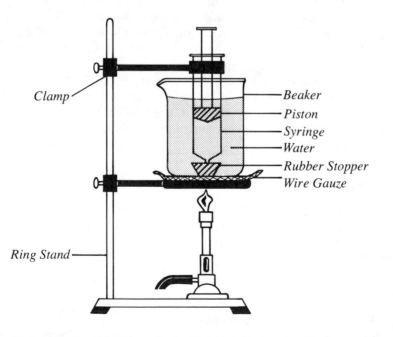

Fig. 41-1 Apparatus for Measuring the Relationship between the Volume and the Temperature of a Given Amount of Gas

C. Push the piston into the syringe, and release it, several times. Then read the volume of the trapped gas. Stir the water to ensure that the water temperature is uniform, and measure the temperature of the water.

D. Adjust the temperature in the beaker by heating it with a burner. Warm the water in 10-15°C increments. Measure the volume of the trapped gas for each recorded temperature. In each case, push the piston into the syringe, and release it, several times before you measure the volume of the trapped gas. Stir the water in the beaker to ensure a uniform temperature for each temperature measurement.

Concluding Questions

(1) What is the effect of an increase in temperature on the volume of the trapped gas?

(2) What can you say about the constancy of the V/t ratios?

(3) What can you say about the constancy of the V/T ratios?

(4) What type of graph is obtained if volume (vertical axis) is plotted against temperature (horizontal axis)? Use the temperature scale (Celsius or Kelvin) which gives the most constant volume-to-temperature ratio.

(5) What type of graph is obtained if volume (vertical axis) is plotted against the reciprocal of temperature? Use the same temperature scale you used in question 4.

(6) What is the relationship between the temperature and the volume of a given quantity of a gas at a constant pressure?

(7) Why was it necessary that pressure remain constant during this experiment?

42 Percentage of Oxygen in Air

Purpose

To determine the percentage of oxygen in the air by volume.

Introduction

Lavoisier first determned the percentage of oxygen in the air by heating mercury in air in a closed container. The mercury combined with the oxygen in the air to form mercury calx [mercury(II) oxide]. In this experiment you will use a mixture of pyrogallol and sodium hydroxide to react with the oxygen and remove it from an accurately measured sample of air in a stoppered gas measuring tube. Since the oxygen part of the air in the tube is removed, there is a partial vacuum in the gas measuring tube. When the stopper is removed under water, the water rushes in to replace the missing oxygen. The difference between the original volume of trapped air and the new volume equals the volume of lost oxygen.

Apparatus

battery jar	10 mL graduated cylinder
gas measuring tube	rubber stopper
small test tube	crucible tongs

Materials

pyrogallol	1.0 mol/L sodium hydroxide

Procedure

A. Prepare a data table as shown. Record all experimental results in the data table as soon as you obtain them. Complete the remainder of the table as soon as you have enough data to do so.

Data Table 42-1

Volume of free space	_____ mL
Initial volume of air	50.0 mL
Volume of gas remaining	_____ mL
Volume of oxygen removed	_____ mL

B. Fill a battery jar with water.

C. Fill a gas measuring tube with water to the 50 mL mark. Notice that there is still free space in the tube. To measure the volume of this space, close the gas measuring tube with a rubber stopper and turn it upside down (Fig. 42-1a). Measure and record the volume of free space in the tube. In part E, when a volume of sodium hydroxide equal to this volume of free space is placed in the tube, and the tube is stoppered (Fig. 42-1b), 50.0 mL of air will be trapped in the tube. Pour the water out of the gas measuring tube.

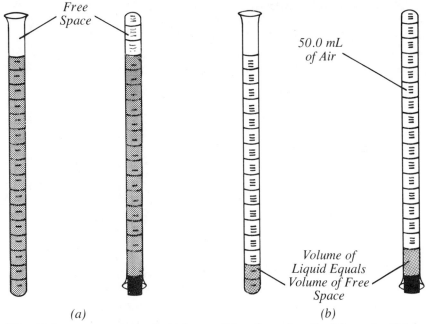

(a)   *(b)*

Fig. 42-1 (a) Determining the Volume of Free Space in a Gas Measuring Tube Which Contains 50.0 mL of Liquid
(b) Trapping 50.0 mL of Air in a Gas Measuring Tube

D. Measure into a small test tube 0.5 g of pyrogallol (estimated by comparison with 0.5 g in a display test tube). Add the pyrogallol to the gas measuring tube.

E. Measure in a graduated cylinder the required volume of sodium hydroxide solution determined in part C. Pour the sodium hydroxide solution into the gas measuring tube and close the tube quickly with a rubber stopper. Turn the tube upside down 4 or 5 times to ensure that the pyrogallol and the sodium hydroxide are well mixed. Wait three minutes.

F. Place the stoppered end of the tube under the water in the battery jar and remove the stopper using crucible tongs.

G. Wait several minutes for the gas in the tube to come to room temperature. Adjust the tube so that the level of the water inside the tube is the same as the level of water in the battery jar. This ensures that the pressure of the gas in the tube continues to equal atmospheric pressure. Measure the volume of the gas remaining in the gas measuring tube.

Concluding Questions

(1) Why is it not necessary to measure the pyrogallol accurately?

(2) Why are the two operations described in part F performed in the indicated order rather than in the reverse order?

(3) Why do you think it is necessary to wait for the gas in the tube to come to room temperature?

(4) What is the percentage of oxygen in the air by volume as calculated from your data?

$$\%O_2 = \frac{\text{Volume of Oxygen Removed}}{\text{Volume of Air}} \times 100$$

(5) If the accepted value for the percentage of oxygen in air by volume is 20.9%, what is the percent error in your answer to question 4?

(6) If the rubber stopper had not been inserted tightly into the gas measuring tube in part E, would there have been any effect on your results? If so, what would have been the effect?

(7) What are two other elements that each contribute a significant percentage to the volume of air? What is the actual percentage by volume of each of these two elements in air?

(8) In a table of the percentages by volume of the constituents of air, water vapour is usually omitted. What do you suppose is the reason for this?

43 Reaction of Hydrochloric Acid with Magnesium

Purpose

To determine the volume of hydrogen gas produced when a given quantity of magnesium reacts with excess hydrochloric acid.

Introduction

In this experiment a given mass of magnesium will be allowed to react with excess hydrochloric acid in a gas measuring tube. The volume of hydrogen produced will be measured and the room temperature and pressure will be recorded.

Since the hydrogen gas will be collected over water, the hydrogen will be mixed with water vapour. The pressure of the dry hydrogen gas can be calculated by subtracting the water vapour pressure from the room pressure. Water vapour pressures at various temperatures are found in Table 43-1.

Table 43-1 Water Vapour Pressure

°C	kPa	°C	kPa
15	1.71	23	2.81
16	1.82	24	2.98
17	1.94	25	3.17
18	2.06	26	3.36
19	2.20	27	3.57
20	2.34	28	3.78
21	2.49	29	4.00
22	2.64	30	4.24

Knowing the volume, pressure, and temperature of dry hydrogen gas, you can correct the volume to STP. The mass of magnesium used can be converted to the number of moles of magnesium used. The volume of dry hydrogen at STP produced by one mole of magnesium can then be calculated.

Apparatus

ruler	10 mL graduated cylinder
copper wire	one-hole rubber stopper, size 00
gas measuring tube	battery jar
ring stand	thermometer
buret clamp	barometer
400 mL beaker	

Materials

magnesium ribbon	6 mol/L hydrochloric acid

Procedure

A. Prepare a data table as shown. Record all experimental results in the data table as soon as you obtain them. Complete the remainder of the data table as soon as you have enough data to do so.

Data Table 43-1

Mass of one metre of Mg	_____ g
Length of Mg used	_____ cm
Mass of Mg used	_____ g
Moles of Mg used	_____ mol
Room temperature	_____ °C
Room pressure	_____ kPa
Temperature of the water	_____ °C
Volume of hydrogen gas and water vapour collected	_____ L

B. Obtain a piece of magnesium ribbon about 3-4 cm long. Measure this ribbon as precisely as possible with a ruler. The magnesium ribbon is assumed to be uniform in thickness and width. You will be told the mass of one metre of the ribbon. From this you can calculate the mass of your piece of ribbon.

C. Roll the piece of magnesium ribbon into a tight coil. Use fine copper wire to build a cage around the magnesium (Fig. 43-1).

The cage should have no large openings through which small pieces of magnesium ribbon could pass. This copper cage must be small enough to fit into the gas measuring tube. Leave enough extra copper wire attached to the cage to act as a handle.

Fig. 43-1 Copper Cage Containing Magnesium

D. Set up a ring stand and buret clamp, and fill a 400 mL beaker about two-thirds full of water. Figure 43-2 shows what the apparatus will look like when the gas measuring tube is in position.

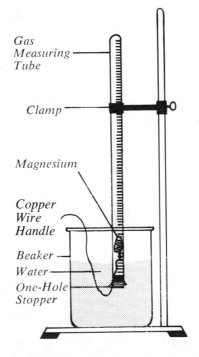

Fig. 43-2 Apparatus for Determining the Volume of Hydrogen Produced by a Given Quantity of Magnesium

E. Carefully pour 10 mL of 6 mol/L hydrochloric acid into the gas measuring tube. Slowly fill the tube with tap water. Rinse down any acid that may be on the walls of the tube but try to avoid stirring up the acid layer in the bottom of the tube. The tube should be completely filled with water so that when a one-hole stopper (size 00) is placed in the tube a little water will be forced out. Any bubbles sticking to the walls of the tube may be dislodged by tapping the tube gently.

F. Holding the wire handle, lower the copper cage containing the magnesium into the water to a depth of about 5 cm. Place the one-hole stopper into the mouth of the tube so that the wire handle is caught between the glass and the stopper.

G. Cover the hole in the stopper with your finger and invert the tube. Place the inverted tube in the beaker of water. Clamp the tube in position (Fig. 43-2). The hydrochloric acid will eventually reach the magnesium ribbon and a reaction will occur. There is no danger that the acid will reach the stopper before you remove your finger.

H. When the magnesium ribbon has disappeared and the reaction has finished, wait for 5 min to allow the gas in the tube to come to room temperature. Dislodge any gas bubbles that are sticking to the walls of the tube by tapping the tube.

I. Cover the hole in the stopper with your finger and transfer the tube to a battery jar or a large graduated cylinder filled with water. Remove your finger and adjust the tube so that the level of the water inside the tube is the same as the level of the water outside the tube. When the two levels are equal, the pressure on the water outside the tube (room pressure) equals the pressure on the water inside the tube caused by the gases in the tube. Read the gas volume. Drain and clean the gas measuring tube.

J. Measure the room temperature and the temperature of the water in the battery jar or graduated cylinder. Use this latter temperature to obtain the water vapour pressure from Table 43-1. Obtain the room pressure.

Concluding Questions

(1) In part H, why is it necessary to wait for 5 min to allow the gas in the tube to come to room temperature?

(2) What was the water vapour pressure at the measured water temperature?

(3) What was the pressure exerted by the hydrogen alone?

(4) What volume would the dry hydrogen gas occupy at STP?

(5) Based on the results of this experiment, what volume of hydrogen at STP would have been produced by one mole of magnesium?

(6) Given that one mole of magnesium produces one mole of hydrogen gas, what is the molar volume of hydrogen gas at STP determined in this experiment?

(7) What is the percent difference between your answer and the accepted value for the molar volume of hydrogen gas at STP?

44 The Molar Mass of a Volatile Liquid

Purpose

To determine the molar mass of a volatile liquid.

Introduction

In this experiment, you will determine the molar mass of a compound by using a modification of a historical method. This method can be used with volatile (easily evaporated) liquids. The volatile liquid is placed in a flask. The top of the flask is covered by a cap with a small hole. The flask is heated in a hot water bath of known temperature. The liquid evaporates, its vapour fills the flask, and excess vapour exits through the small hole in the cap. When the flask is cooled to room temperature, the vapour remaining in it condenses. The mass of this condensed liquid equals the mass of the vapour that filled the flask at the higher temperature of the hot water bath. The volume of the flask equals the volume of the vapour at room pressure and the temperature of the hot water bath. The volume that this mass of vapour would occupy at STP can be calculated. Since one mole of an ideal gas occupies 22.4 L at STP, the mass of one mole (molar mass) of the volatile liquid can be determined.

Apparatus

125 mL Erlenmeyer flask	iron ring
10 mL graduated cylinder	wire gauze
fine pin	burner
buret clamp	250 mL graduated cylinder
ring stand	600 mL beaker

Materials

aluminum foil	boiling chips
volatile liquid	

Procedure

A. Prepare a data table as shown. Record all experimental results in the data table as soon as you obtain them. Complete the remainder of the data table as soon as you have enough data to do so.

Data Table 44-1

Mass of flask and foil together	_____ g
Mass of flask, foil, and condensed liquid	_____ g
Mass of condensed liquid = mass of vapour	_____ g
Temperature	_____ °C
Barometric pressure	_____ kPa
Volume of flask	_____ L

B. Determine the mass of a 5 cm square of aluminum foil and a 125 mL Erlenmeyer flask together.

C. Pour 3 mL of an unknown volatile liquid into the flask. Prepare a cap for the flask by placing the aluminum foil on the mouth of the flask and folding it tightly about the mouth of the flask. Use a pin to make a *tiny* hole in the center of the foil. The hole should be as small as possible.

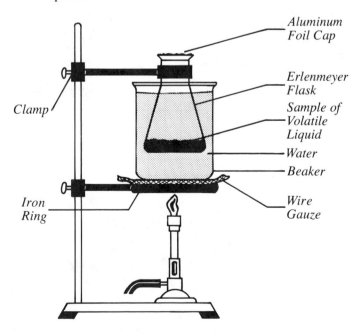

Fig. 44-1 Apparatus for Evaporating a Volatile Liquid

D. Clamp the flask to a ring stand and suspend it in a 600 mL beaker. Tilt the flask slightly so that you can see the liquid. Add a few boiling chips to the beaker and pour water into the beaker so that the flask is surrounded with water (Fig. 44-1).

E. Heat the beaker until the last traces of the liquid have gone from the flask. (It is not necessary to heat the water to a vigorous boil.) When all of the liquid has evaporated from the flask, immediately remove the flask from the beaker and measure the temperature of the water bath. Allow the flask to cool to room temperature.

F. Wipe the outside of the flask, including the cap, with a paper towel to dry it. Be sure to remove any drops of water which may be trapped between the foil and the glass. Determine the total mass of the flask, the cap, and the condensed liquid.

G. Remove the cap from the flask and fill the flask to the top with tap water. Measure the volume of the flask by pouring the water into a 250 mL graduated cylinder.

Concluding Questions

(1) What would be the volume of the vapour at STP?

(2) What is the density of the vapour in grams per litre at STP?

(3) What is the calculated molar mass of your unknown?

(4) What is the molecular mass of your unknown?

(5) If you had made a rather large hole in the foil cap, what effect would it have had on your calculated molar mass?

45 Preparation of t-Butyl Chloride

Purpose

To prepare t-butyl chloride.

Introduction

In this experiment, you will prepare the organic compound t-butyl chloride by reacting concentrated hydrochloric acid with t-butyl alcohol according to the following equation:

$$H_3C-\underset{\underset{CH_3}{|}}{\overset{\overset{CH_3}{|}}{C}}-OH + HCl \rightarrow H_3C-\underset{\underset{CH_3}{|}}{\overset{\overset{CH_3}{|}}{C}}-Cl + H_2O$$

Excess hydrochloric acid must be neutralized and the water must be removed in order to purify the t-butyl chloride.

Apparatus

150 mm test tubes (3)   one-hole rubber stopper
10 mL graduated cylinder   glass tubing
pipet   buret clamp
pipet bulb   ring stand
filter paper   600 mL beakers (2)
funnel   burner

Materials

t-butyl alcohol   0.6 mol/L sodium hydrogen
12 mol/L hydrochloric acid   carbonate
anhydrous calcium sulfate

Procedure

A. Place 5 mL of *t*-butyl alcohol into a 150 mm test tube. Carefully add 10 mL of 12 mol/L hydrochloric acid in a fume hood or well ventilated area. CAUTION: 12 mol/L hydrochloric acid can cause severe skin damage, and the fumes of this acid can attack the mucous membranes. *(1) What do you observe?*

B. Allow the reaction to take place for 8 min. *(2) What do you observe in the test tube during this time?*

C. After the chemicals have reacted for 8 min, remove the lower aqueous layer with a pipet and discard it.

D. Add 5 mL of distilled water to the test tube and shake gently to allow the two layers to mix. Remove the water layer as in part C. Repeat this process of adding and then removing water once more.

E. Wash the organic contents of the test tube by adding 5 mL of 0.6 mol/L sodium hydrogen carbonate and shaking the test tube gently. Remove as much of the lower aqueous layer as possible, using a pipet.

F. Add about 0.25 g of anhydrous calcium sulfate to help remove traces of water in the test tube. Stopper the test tube and shake it gently for 2 min.

G. Filter the liquid in the test tube into another clean, dry 150 mm test tube. Set up a distillation apparatus as shown in Fig. 45-1, and distill the liquid into another clean, dry test tube. Examine the distillation product. *(3) What do you observe?*

Concluding Questions

(1) In part A, what evidence is there that a chemical reaction is taking place?

(2) In part B, what evidence is there that the reaction is complete after 8 min?

(3) Which is more dense, water or *t*-butyl chloride? How do you know?

(4) What properties of *t*-butyl chloride did you observe?

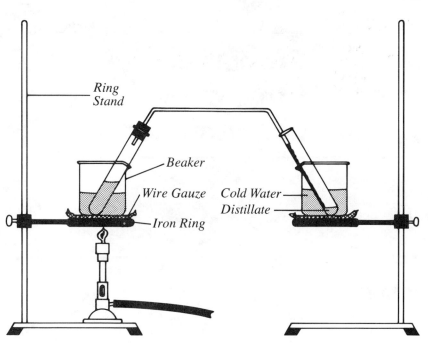

Fig. 45-1 Distillation Apparatus

46 Preparation of Ethanol by Fermentation

Purpose

To prepare ethanol and identify some of its properties.

Introduction

When grain, tubers, and fruits ferment, the carbohydrates in them are converted by a series of reactions to ethanol, CH_3CH_2OH. Various enzymes contained in yeast speed up the reactions involved.

Prior to this experiment your teacher mixed a cake of yeast with sugar and warm water. This mixture was added to a large bottle containing 2500 mL of warm water and 500 mL of molasses. This mixture has been quietly fermenting for several days.

In this experiment, you will distill the ethanol from the fermentation mixture, and then you will determine some of the properties of the purified ethanol.

Apparatus

250 mL distillation flask or
   Florence flask
buret clamp
condenser clamp
thermometer
bent glass tube (60°)
two-hole rubber stopper for flask
wire gauze
iron ring

ring stands (2)
burner
condenser
one-hole rubber stopper
   for condenser
pieces of rubber tubing (2)
10 mL graduated cylinder
evaporating dishes (3)
large watch glass

Materials

molasses and yeast mixture   wooden splints
boiling chips

Procedure

A. In a 250 mL flask place 150 mL of the fermented liquid and a boiling chip. Arrange the apparatus as shown in Fig. 46-1. Run cold water through the condenser as shown. Heat the solution with a burner, and collect the distillate in a 10 mL graduated cylinder. *(1) At what temperature does the first drop of distillate fall into the receiver?*

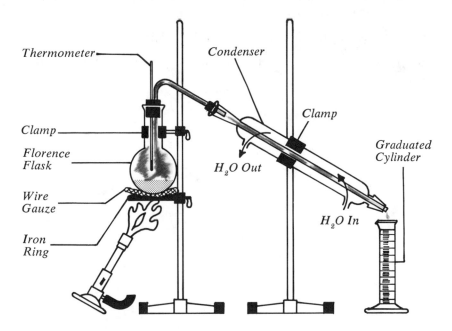

Fig. 46-1 Apparatus for the Distillation of Ethanol

B. Collect three 10 mL portions of distillate and place them in evaporating dishes. *(2) What are the temperatures at the beginning and end of each 10 mL collection? (3) What is the odour of each portion?* Bring a burning splint to the surface of each portion. *(4) Does any portion ignite?* If so, extinguish the flame immediately by covering the dish with a watch glass.

C. Empty the distillation flask. Place in it the three combined portions of distillate and a fresh boiling chip. Collect a 10 mL portion of distillate. *(5) What are the temperatures at the beginning and at the end of this distillation? (6) What is the odour of this portion of distillate? (7) Does this portion ignite when tested with a burning splint as described in part B?*

Concluding Questions

(1) What are the properties of ethanol that you were able to observe?

(2) If any portion of distillate ignited, what was the boiling temperature range of the portion which burned?

(3) What is the chemical equation for the preparation of ethanol from sucrose $(C_{12}H_{22}O_{11})$?

(4) What is the chemical equation for the combustion of ethanol?

(5) What are the most important industrial uses of ethanol?

47 Percentage of Acetic Acid in Vinegar

Purpose

To determine the percentage by mass of acetic acid in vinegar.

Introduction

Acetic acid is produced by the bacterial oxidation of ethanol. Apple cider is often the source of such ethanol. The process stops when the concentration of acetic acid becomes large enough to prevent the bacteria from continuing the oxidation of ethanol. The resulting solution of acetic acid is called vinegar.

In this experiment you will titrate the acetic acid in a known mass of vinegar with sodium hydroxide solution of a known concentration. The sodium hydroxide will neutralize the acetic acid. Phenolphthalein is added to indicate the point at which the acetic acid has been completely neutralized by the sodium hydroxide.

A knowledge of the concentration (moles per litre) and the volume (litres) of the sodium hydroxide required to neutralize the acetic acid enables us to calculate the number of moles of sodium hydroxide used. Since acetic acid has one ionizable hydrogen atom per molecule, one mole of sodium hydroxide will neutralize one mole of acetic acid:

$$NaOH(aq) + HC_2H_3O_2(aq) \rightarrow NaC_2H_3O_2(aq) + H_2O(\ell)$$

Hence, the number of moles of acetic acid present in the vinegar can be obtained and used to calculate the mass of acetic acid in the known mass of vinegar.

Apparatus

150 mL beaker
50 mL buret
buret clamp
250 mL beaker

ring stand
250 mL Erlenmeyer flasks (2)
50 mL graduated cylinder

Materials

vinegar
1.00 mol/L sodium hydroxide

phenolphthalein solution

Procedure

A. Prepare a data table as shown. Record all experimental results in the data table as soon as you obtain them. Complete the remainder of the data table as soon as you have enough data to do so.

Data Table 47-1

Measurements and Results	#1	#2
Mass of flask and vinegar	———— g	———— g
Mass of empty flask	———— g	———— g
Mass of vinegar	———— g	———— g
Final reading of buret	———— mL	———— mL
Initial reading of buret	———— mL	———— mL
Volume of NaOH used	———— mL	———— mL
Moles of NaOH used	———— mol	———— mol
Moles of acetic acid in vinegar	———— mol	———— mol
Mass of acetic acid in vinegar	———— g	———— g
Percentage of acetic acid in vinegar	———— %	———— %

B. Label two Erlenmeyer flasks 1 and 2. Determine the mass of each flask. Rinse a graduated cylinder with 5 mL of vinegar, then measure 20 mL of vinegar into each flask. Determine the total mass of each flask containing the vinegar. Add 1 drop of phenolphthalein solution to each flask. *(1) What is the color of phenolphthalein in vinegar?*

C. Obtain about 120 mL of sodium hydroxide solution in a 150 mL beaker. Rinse the buret with about 10 mL of this solution and let the liquid drain through the buret tip into an empty 250 mL beaker. Repeat this procedure twice more. Refill the buret so that the meniscus of the solution is above the zero mark, and fasten the buret to a ring stand with a buret clamp. Let some of the sodium hydroxide solution run rapidly from the buret to expel all air bubbles from the tip and to bring the level of the solution down to the calibrated region of the buret. If there is a drop of solution hanging on the buret tip, remove it by touching the drop to the inside wall of the 250 mL beaker. Hold a piece of white paper behind the meniscus, and read the initial volume of the sodium hydroxide solution at the bottom of the meniscus. Your eye must be at the same level as the meniscus, as shown in Fig. 5-1.

D. Place one of the Erlenmeyer flasks under the tip of the buret. A piece of white paper placed under the flask will make it easier to see the colour changes. While continuously swirling the flask to ensure thorough mixing, run in the sodium hydroxide solution from the buret until the colour which forms as the sodium hydroxide hits the solution does not disappear quickly. *(2) What colour change do you observe?* Then add the sodium hydroxide solution more slowly, finally adding it drop by drop until 1 drop is sufficient to cause a permanent colour change. This colour change indicates that enough sodium hydroxide has been added to neutralize the acetic acid in the vinegar. Read the final volume of the sodium hydroxide solution. The volume of sodium hydroxide used in the titration is measured in millilitres, and it must be converted to litres in order to complete the calculations.

E. Refill the buret and repeat the titration using the second flask.

Concluding Questions

(1) If 10.35 g of vinegar required 31.44 mL of 0.347 mol/L sodium hydroxide in a titration, what was the percentage by mass of acetic acid in the vinegar?

(2) If 25.41 mL of acetic acid solution is neutralized by 35.47 mL of 0.255 mol/L sodium hydroxide, what is the concentration of the acetic acid?

48 Esters

Purpose

To study a method for making esters, and to study some of their properties.

Introduction

The reaction of a carboxylic acid with an alcohol results in the formation of an ester:

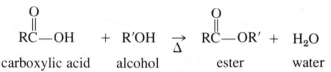

Many esters are pleasant-smelling substances and are, in fact, responsible for the fragrances of many flowers and fruits. In this experiment you will prepare several esters and compare their odours with the odours of their components. This is accomplished by pouring the reaction mixtures into cold water. The polar carboxylic acids and alcohols tend to dissolve in the water. The less polar esters tend to be insoluble and to float on top of the water, where their odour is more easily detected.

Apparatus

250 mL beaker	wire gauze
burner	medicine dropper
ring stand	evaporating dish
iron ring	150 mm test tubes (4)

Materials

ethanol	salicylic acid
acetic acid	methanol
3-methyl-l-butanol	concentrated sulfuric acid

Procedure

A. Heat 200 mL of water in a 250 mL beaker to the boiling point. While the water is heating, label four clean, dry test tubes A, B, C, D.

B. In each of test tubes A and B place 10 drops of ethanol and 10 drops of acetic acid. In test tube C place 10 drops of 3-methyl-1-butanol and 10 drops of acetic acid. In test tube D place enough salicylic acid to fill it 1 cm deep. Add 3 mL of methanol. Place 3 drops of concentrated sulfuric acid in each of test tubes B and C, and 5 drops of sulfuric acid in tube D. CAUTION: Concentrated sulfuric acid is very corrosive to skin and clothing. Mix the contents of each test tube well. *(1) Describe as closely as possible the odour of the contents of each of the tubes.*

C. Place all four test tubes in the boiling water for 5 min. Then pour the contents of test tube A into an evaporating dish half-full of cold water. *(2) Describe the odour of the contents of the evaporating dish.*

D. Rinse the evaporating dish and pour the contents of test tube B into the evaporating dish half-full of cold water. *(3) Describe the odour of the contents of the dish. (4) Do the odours in test tubes A and B differ from each other? (5) If so, in what way do they differ?*

E. Again, rinse the evaporating dish and pour the contents of test tube C into an evaporating dish half-full of cold water. *(6) Describe the odour.*

F. Finally, pour the contents of test tube D into an evaporating dish half-full of cold water. *(7) Describe the odour.*

Concluding Questions

(1) What can you say about the effect of sulfuric acid on the reaction between ethanol and acetic acid? Explain your answer.

(2) What substances produce the odours in test tubes B, C, and D?

(3) What are the chemical equations for the reactions that occurred in each case?

(4) What substance, besides a carboxylic acid and an alcohol, is required to prepare an ester? How do you know?

(5) How would you prepare an ester from acetic acid and 1-butanol? Give an equation for the reaction.

(6) On the basis of this experiment, suggest a likely commercial use for esters.

49 Carbohydrates

Purpose

To study the reactions of different classes of carbohydrates with specific reagents, and to use the results of these reactions to identify an unknown carbohydrate.

Introduction

Carbohydrates react with many different reagents, usually to give coloured products. The specific reactants are named after the chemists who discovered them, and in many cases the exact structure of the products is still not known. The value of the tests lies in the fact that different results are obtained depending on the nature of the carbohydrate, that is, on whether it is a monosaccharide or a polysaccharide, an aldose or a ketose, a pentose or a hexose, and so on.

You will be given an aqueous solution of an unknown carbohydrate which is either ribose, glucose, fructose, or starch. Once you have determined the effects of each reagent on known compounds, you can use this knowledge to identify your unknown.

When running a test for the first time it is desirable to run a "control" or "blank" which contains no carbohydrate. This shows what the reagent alone looks like and gives a basis for comparison when trying to decide whether the colour or some other property of a solution has changed. Also, when attempting to identify an unknown, it is a desirable practice to run known solutions (as well as blanks) along with the unknown. Exact times required for reaction, the colour produced, and other variables may depend on the age of the reagent, concentration of solution, and other factors.

Apparatus

medicine dropper	10 mL graduated cylinder
150 mm test tubes (8)	400 mL beaker

wire gauze   burner
iron ring   evaporating dish
ring stand   filter paper

Materials

1% ribose solution   1% unknown carbohydrate solution
1% glucose solution   Bial's reagent
1% fructose solution   Seliwanoff's reagent
1% starch solution   0.05% iodine solution

Procedure

A.   Prepare a large data table as shown. Record all experimental
results in the data table as soon as you obtain them.

Data Table 49-1

Carbohydrate	TEST		
	Bial	Seliwanoff	Iodine
Ribose			
Glucose			
Fructose			
Starch			
Unknown			
Blank (water)			

BIAL'S TEST

B.   For this part you will test solutions of ribose, glucose, an
unknown carbohydrate, and a blank. First, place about 200 mL of
tap water in a 400 mL beaker and heat it to boiling on the ring
stand. While the water is heating, place about 1 mL (20 drops) of
each substance to be tested in separate test tubes. Add approximately 2 mL of Bial's reagent to each test tube. Mix well and
place them in the water bath when it reaches the boiling point.
Observe any colour changes during 15 min of heating. *(1) What is
a negative result (obtained from the blank)? (2) Which of the two
known carbohydrates gives a negative result? (3) Which gives a
positive result? (4) What is a positive result?*

SELIWANOFF'S TEST

C.   For this part you will use solutions of glucose, fructose, an
unknown carbohydrate, and a blank. To 2 mL of Seliwanoff's
reagent in separate test tubes add 4 drops of the solution to be

tested. Mix well and place in the boiling water bath. Record the time required for any changes in colour or transparency to occur. Leave tubes in the water bath for 10 min before recording a negative result. *(5) What is a negative result? (6) Which of the two known carbohydrates gives a negative result? (7) Which gives a positive result? (8) What is a positive result?*

THE IODINE TEST

D. For this part you will use solutions of glucose, starch, an unknown carbohydrate, and a blank. In an evaporating dish or spot plate add a drop of iodine solution to 5 drops of each separate solution. *(9) What is a negative result? (10) Which of the two known carbohydrates gives a negative result? (11) Which gives a positive result? (12) What is a positive result?*

Concluding Questions

(1) In what way do glucose and ribose differ (i.e., aldose vs. ketose, pentose vs. hexose, monosaccharide vs. polysaccharide, etc.)?

(2) What class of carbohydrate is Bial's test useful in distinguishing?

(3) In what way do glucose and fructose differ?

(4) What class of carbohydrate is Seliwanoff's test useful in distinguishing?

(5) In what way do glucose and starch differ?

(6) What kind of carbohydrate is the iodine test useful in distinguishing?

(7) Is your unknown carbohydrate a ketose? How do you know?

(8) Is it a pentose or a carbohydrate with more carbon atoms?

(9) Is it a monosaccharide or a polysaccharide? How do you know?

(10) What carbohydrate is present in your unknown solution?

(11) Suppose your chemistry teacher had prepared solutions of ribose, glucose, and fructose for this experiment and a student had accidentally mixed up the bottles before they could be properly labelled. What is the minimum number of tests you would have had to perform in order to label the three bottles correctly? Describe what tests you would perform and the information you would obtain from each.

50 Enzymes of Digestion — Hydrolysis of Starch

Purpose

To study the ability of amylase to catalyze the hydrolysis of starch.

Introduction

The molecules of the food we eat are converted by the process of digestion into molecules that the body can use as sources of energy or as starting materials for the building of body tissues. Many different enzymes are involved in the digestion process.

An enzyme called amylase found in saliva catalyzes the hydrolysis of starch in the food we eat and thus initiates the process of digestion. In this experiment you will investigate the ability of amylase to catalyze the hydrolysis of starch molecules.

Starch is a polymer consisting of many glucose units joined together. The hydrolysis of starch produces progressively smaller fragments, eventually yielding molecules of glucose and maltose (a disaccharide consisting of two glucose units joined together).

Apparatus

150 mm test tubes (6)
10 mL graduated cylinder
400 mL beaker
ring stand
iron ring
stirring rod

wire gauze
burner
test tube holder
medicine dropper
filter paper

Materials

starch

iodine reagent

amylase solution

maltose solution

glucose solution

Procedure

A. Place about 1 g of starch in a test tube. Make a suspension by adding 10 mL of water in 2-3 mL portions, stirring after each addition. Heat the mixture in a boiling water bath for 5 min, stirring the starch suspension from time to time. *(1) What changes do you observe in the starch mixture?* Remove the tube from the water bath. Cool the contents to room temperature by holding the tube under cold tap water. Place 3 drops of the solution in a clean test tube and add 2 drops of the iodine reagent. View the result against a piece of white filter paper. *(2) What do you observe?*

B. Add about 1 mL (20 drops) of the amylase solution to the starch mixture and shake to mix. Note the time. Then let the solution sit, and proceed to part C.

C. Place 3 drops of a solution of maltose in a test tube and add 2 drops of the iodine reagent. View the result against a white background. *(3) What do you observe?* In the same way, test 3 drops of a solution of glucose with a drop of the iodine reagent. *(4) What do you observe?*

D. Ten minutes after you have added the amylase solution, retest the starch solution of part B with the iodine reagent (as you did in part A). *(5) What do you observe?* Continue testing the solution with the iodine reagent every 5 min until the end of the period or until no colour is generated by the addition of the iodine reagent. *(6) What is the result of each test?* Present your answer in the form of a table.

Concluding Questions

(1) How can the iodine reagent be used as a test for starch?

(2) How do you explain the results of the successive tests in part D?

(3) If you chewed soda crackers rapidly and swallowed them with a dry mouth, would the starch in them still have a chance of being digested?

EXPERIMENT

51 Analysis of an Antacid

Purpose

To determine how many times its own mass in excess stomach acid an antacid tablet will consume.

Introduction

The human stomach contains hydrochloric acid which acts directly on ingested food and activates the enzyme pepsin for digesting proteins. Stomach acid is approximately 0.1 mol/L hydrochloric acid. Excessive secretion of stomach acid causes the acidity of the stomach to become so great that the pH of the contents of the stomach falls below 3.0. Antacids are compounds that reduce the amount of acid in the stomach. An antacid is said to consume excess stomach acid when it maintains the pH of the stomach at 3.0 even if more acid is secreted into the stomach.

In this experiment, 0.100 mol/L hydrochloric acid is used to simulate stomach acid. A crushed antacid tablet is added to 100 g of the stomach acid. An acid-base indicator (bromophenol blue) which changes colour in the pH range of 3.0 to 4.6 is added to the acid-antacid mixture. The antacid will neutralize much of the stomach acid, but the colour of the bromophenol blue indicates that the pH remains below 3.0. That is, there is still an excess of stomach acid. Sodium hydroxide having the same concentration as the hydrochloric acid is then titrated into the mixture until the bromophenol blue changes colour. The volume of sodium hydroxide used in the titration will neutralize the same volume of hydrochloric acid. The sodium hydroxide neutralizes the hydrochloric acid which the antacid leaves unreacted. The larger the quantity of hydrochloric acid neutralized by the antacid, the smaller the quantity of sodium hydroxide required to neutralize the remaining acid.

161

Since one millilitre of the 0.100 mol/L hydrochloric acid has a mass of one gram, the volume of acid (in millilitres) neutralized by the sodium hydroxide is numerically equal to the mass of acid (in grams) neutralized by the sodium hydroxide. We can calculate the mass of excess stomach acid neutralized by the antacid:

$$\begin{array}{l} \text{Mass of acid} \\ \text{neutralized by antacid} \end{array} + \begin{array}{l} \text{Mass of acid} \\ \text{neutralized by NaOH} \end{array} = \text{Total mass of acid (100 g)}$$

$$\therefore \begin{array}{l} \text{Mass of acid} \\ \text{neutralized by antacid} \end{array} = 100\,\text{g} - \begin{array}{l} \text{Mass of acid} \\ \text{neutralized by NaOH} \end{array}$$

We can then calculate the number of times its own mass in excess stomach acid an antacid tablet will consume:

$$\frac{\text{Mass of acid neutralized by antacid}}{\text{Mass of antacid used}} = \begin{array}{l} \text{Number of times its own mass an} \\ \text{antacid tablet will neutralize} \end{array}$$

Apparatus

100 mL graduated cylinder	buret clamp
250 mL Erlenmeyer flasks (3)	ring stand
mortar and pestle	150 mL beaker
50 mL buret	250 mL beaker

Materials

0.100 mol/L hydrochloric acid	4% bromophenol blue solution
antacid tablets	0.100 mol/L sodium hydroxide

Procedure

A. Prepare a data table as shown. Record all experimental results in the data table as soon as you obtain them. Complete the remainder of the data table as soon as you have enough data to do so.

B. Carefully measure 100 mL (100 g) of hydrochloric acid and place this amount in a 250 mL Erlenmeyer flask.

C. Obtain an antacid tablet. Several brands will be tested by the students in your class. Crush the antacid tablet using a mortar and pestle. Determine the mass of the crushed tablet and transfer it to the Erlenmeyer flask.

D. Dissolve the antacid in the hydrochloric acid. Some of the inert ingredients used in making the tablet will not dissolve, and the

Data Table 51-1

Measurements and Results	#1	#2	#3
Mass of hydrochloric acid	100 g	100 g	100 g
Final reading of buret	_____ mL	_____ mL	_____ mL
Initial reading of buret	_____ mL	_____ mL	_____ mL
Volume of NaOH used	_____ mL	_____ mL	_____ mL
Volume of acid neutralized by NaOH	_____ mL	_____ mL	_____ mL
Mass of acid neutralized by NaOH	_____ g	_____ g	_____ g
Mass of acid neutralized by antacid	_____ g	_____ g	_____ g
Mass of antacid used	_____ g	_____ g	_____ g
Number of times its own mass the antacid tablet will neutralize	_____	_____	_____

solution will be cloudy. However, this is not important in this experiment.

E. Add 2 drops of a 4% solution of bromophenol blue in alcohol to the acid-antacid mixture. *(1) What colour of the bromophenol blue indicator shows that excess acid is present?*

F. Obtain about 120 mL of sodium hydroxide solution in a 150 mL beaker. Rinse the buret with about 10 mL of this solution and let the liquid drain through the buret tip into an empty 250 mL beaker. Repeat this procedure twice more. Refill the buret so that the meniscus of the solution is above the zero mark, and fasten the buret to a ring stand with a buret clamp. Let some of the sodium hydroxide solution run rapidly from the buret to expel all air bubbles from the tip and to bring the level of the solution down to the calibrated region of the buret. If there is a drop of solution hanging on the buret tip, remove it by touching the drop to the inside wall of the 250 mL beaker. Hold a piece of white paper behind the meniscus, and read the initial volume of the sodium hydroxide at the bottom of the meniscus. Your eye must be at the same level as the meniscus, as shown in Fig. 5-1.

G. Place the Erlenmeyer flask under the tip of the buret. A piece of white paper under the flask will make it easier to see the colour changes. While continuously swirling the flask to ensure thorough mixing, run in the sodium hydroxide from the buret until the solution turns from its original colour through green to blue. The sodium hydroxide should be added until the solution *just* turns blue. Read the final volume of the sodium hydroxide solution.

H. If time permits, refill the buret and repeat the procedure once or twice using antacid tablets of the same brand.

Concluding Questions

(1) What does the colour change observed in part G indicate?

(2) What are the desirable properties of a useful antacid?

(3) If several brands of antacid were tested by the class, which brand consumed the most excess stomach acid per gram of antacid?

(4) If several brands of antacid were tested, which brand was the best buy? That is, which brand consumed the most excess stomach acid per penny of antacid?

52 The Chemistry of Sulfuric Acid

Purpose

To observe some properties of sulfuric acid.

Introduction

Sulfuric acid is the most abundantly produced industrial chemical. It is one of the most important and multifunctional chemicals. In this experiment, you will observe some properties of sulfuric acid and relate these properties to some of its uses.

Apparatus

conductivity apparatus
150 mm test tubes (6)
100 mL beaker
stirring rod

medicine dropper
250 mL beaker
10 mL graduated cylinder

Materials

steel wool
sodium chloride
sugar (sucrose)
iron nail
calcium carbonate
   (marble chips)

18 mol/L sulfuric acid
1 mol/L sulfuric acid
magnesium ribbon
aluminum strips
mossy zinc

Procedure

A. **Teacher demonstration:** Test the conductivity of 50 mL of distilled water contained in a 100 mL beaker. Repeat the conductivity test using 50 mL of 1 mol/L sulfuric acid in place of the distilled water. *(1) What do you observe in each case?*

B. **Teacher demonstration:** Place a few drops of 18 mol/L sulfuric acid on a piece of paper. *(2) What do you observe?* Add sugar to a 250 mL beaker until it is one-third full. Add 10 mL of 18 mol/L sulfuric acid and stir well. *(3) What do you observe?*

C. **Teacher demonstration:** Cover the bottom of a test tube with sodium chloride. Add 5 drops of concentrated sulfuric acid and hold a piece of moistened blue litmus paper in the mouth of the test tube. *(4) What do you observe?*

D. Examine the surface of a grease-free iron nail and a 2 cm piece of magnesium ribbon. *(5) What do you observe in each case?* Place the iron nail in one test tube. Place the piece of magnesium ribbon in a second test tube. Cover each with 1 mol/L sulfuric acid and observe for 3 min. *(6) What do you observe in each case?* Pour off the liquid in the test tube containing the iron nail and examine the nail. *(7) What do you observe?*

E. Place 3 pieces of calcium carbonate in a test tube and add 3 mL of 1 mol/L sulfuric acid. *(8) What do you observe?*

F. Place a piece of mossy zinc in a test tube and add 3 mL of 1 mol/L sulfuric acid. *(9) What do you observe?*

G. Clean the surface of a strip of aluminum with a piece of steel wool. Place the aluminum in a test tube and add 3 mL of 1 mol/L sulfuric acid. *(10) What do you observe?*

Concluding Questions

(1) What chemical properties of sulfuric acid did you observe during this experiment?

(2) Which part or parts of this experiment illustrates the use of sulfuric acid
   (i) in cleaning the surfaces of metals before they are plated?
   (ii) as an electrolyte in car batteries?
   (iii) in the preparation of sulfates such as aluminum sulfate (used in water purification)?
   (iv) as a dehydrating agent (water remover)?
   (v) in the preparation of hydrogen chloride and hydrochloric acid?
   (vi) in the laboratory preparation of hydrogen gas?

(3) What are the balanced chemical equations for the reactions that occur in parts C, D, E, F, and G?

53 Polymers

Purpose

To prepare three polymers and examine their properties.

Introduction

The nylons are a very useful group of condensation polymers, and a wide variety of such polymers has been produced from various diacids (molecules containing 2 carboxyl groups) and diamines (molecules containing 2 amino groups). For example, the reaction between hexamethylenediamine and adipic acid results in the formation of the first of the commercially successful nylons, Nylon 66. (The numbers refer to the numbers of carbon atoms in the amine and the acid, respectively.)

In this experiment, we shall prepare Nylon 610 by using hexamethylenediamine and a 10-carbon acid (sebacic acid). Actually, we shall use the acid chloride (sebacyl chloride) because it reacts more readily than the acid. Hydrogen chloride is formed in this reaction, so a basic solution (sodium carbonate) is added to the reaction mixture to neutralize the acid and to avoid having to use an excess of the expensive diamine.

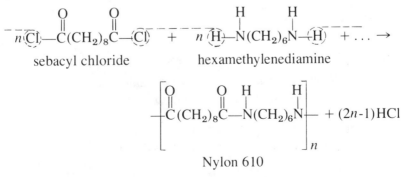

Nylon 610

When phthalic anhydride reacts with ethylene glycol, a polymer with a structure similar to that of Dacron® is formed:

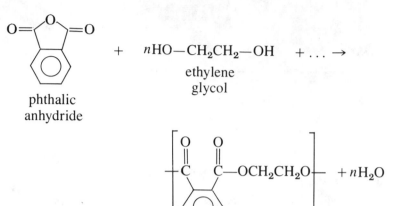

phthalic anhydride

+ nHO—CH₂CH₂—OH   + ... →

ethylene glycol

$+ n\mathrm{H_2O}$

If more than two alcohol groups are present, as in glycerol, the polymer chains may be linked to one another *(cross-linked)* to form a complicated three-dimensional structure. Such structures are usually more rigid than linear structures, and may be more useful for making moulded articles rather than fibres or films. In this experiment, your teacher will react phthalic anhydride with both ethylene glycol and glycerol, and you will then compare the properties of the two polymers formed.

Apparatus

10 mL graduated cylinder
150 mm test tubes (4)
100 mL beakers (2)
forceps or bent copper wire
250 mL beaker

medicine droppers (2)
ring stand
buret clamps (2)
burner

Materials

cyclohexane
5% sebacyl chloride solution
5% hexamethylenediamine
 solution
3 mol/L sodium carbonate
0.2 mol/L acetic acid

phthalic anhydride
sodium acetate
ethylene glycol
glycerol
aluminum foil

Procedure

A. **Teacher demonstration:** In each of two test tubes place 4 g of phthalic anhydride and 0.2 g of sodium acetate. To one tube add 1.5 mL of ethylene glycol. To the other tube add 1.5 mL of glycerol. Clamp both tubes so that they can be heated simultaneously by the same burner. Heat the tubes *gently* until the solutions appear to boil (because of the water formed during the reaction), and maintain the heat for 5 min. Then pour the liquids into two containers made from aluminum foil and allow them to cool. *(1) What do you observe in each case?*

B. Place 2 mL of cyclohexane in a 150 mm test tube. Add 5 mL of water to the test tube. *(2) Are the two liquids miscible? (3) If the two liquids are not miscible, which liquid is in the bottom layer? (4) How do you know?*

C. Place 10 mL of a 5% solution of sebacyl chloride dissolved in cyclohexane in a 100 mL beaker. Place 10 mL of a 5% solution of hexamethylenediamine dissolved in water in a second 100 mL beaker, and add 10 drops of 3 mol/L sodium carbonate.

D. Gently pour the sebacyl chloride solution down the wall of the beaker containing the diamine solution. *(5) What do you observe? (6) If there is any evidence of polymer formation, what is the evidence?*

E. Use a pair of forceps or a bent copper wire to hook the polymer where it has formed. Slowly draw the forceps or copper wire from the beaker so that the polymer is pulled out of the liquid. Wash the nylon polymer in a beaker containing about 200 mL of 0.2 mol/L acetic acid. *(7) What properties of the nylon polymer do you observe?*

Concluding Questions

(1) Why should the nylon be washed in a dilute acid solution?

(2) What type of polymer (condensation or addition) is being formed in part A? In part D?

(3) What are some uses for nylon with which you are familiar?

(4) What are the names of and uses for other polymers with which you are familiar?

(5) What differences did you observe in the properties of the polymers prepared in part A?

Appendix

Solubility Rules for Common Compounds in Water

NO_3^-	All common *nitrates* are soluble.
ClO_3^-	All common *chlorates* are soluble.
$C_2H_3O_2^-$	All *acetates* are soluble. ($AgC_2H_3O_2$ and $Hg_2(C_2H_3O_2)_2$ are only sparingly soluble.)
F^-	All *fluorides* are soluble, except for MnF_2. The compounds BaF_2, CaF_2, CuF_2, FeF_2, FeF_3, PbF_2, MgF_2, NiF_2, SrF_2, and ZnF_2 are sparingly soluble.
Cl^-	All *chlorides* are soluble except for Hg_2Cl_2, AgCl, and $CrCl_3$. The compounds AuCl and $PbCl_2$ are sparingly soluble.
Br^-	All *bromides* are soluble except for Hg_2Br_2 and AgBr. The compounds AuBr and $PtBr_4$ are sparingly soluble.
I^-	All *iodides* are soluble except for BiI_3, CuI, AuI, AuI_3, Hg_2I_2, AgI, and PtI_2. The compounds PbI_2 and HgI_2 are sparingly soluble.
SO_4^{2-}	All *sulfates* are soluble except for $Sb_2(SO_4)_3$, and $BaSO_4$. The compounds $CaSO_4$, $Fe_2(SO_4)_3$, $PbSO_4$, Hg_2SO_4, Ag_2SO_4, and $SrSO_4$ are sparingly soluble.
Na^+	All common *sodium* compounds are soluble.
K^+	All common *potassium* compounds are soluble.
NH_4^+	All common *ammonium* compounds are soluble.
CO_3^{2-}	All *carbonates* are insoluble except for Na_2CO_3, K_2CO_3, and $(NH_4)_2CO_3$. The compounds $BaCO_3$, $CaCO_3$, $FeCO_3$, $MgCO_3$, $MnCO_3$, $NiCO_3$, $SrCO_3$, and $ZnCO_3$ are sparingly soluble.
PO_4^{3-}	All *phosphates* are insoluble except for Na_3PO_4, K_3PO_4, and $(NH_4)_3PO_4$. The compounds $Ca_3(PO_4)_2$, $FePO_4$, $Mg_3(PO_4)_2$, and $Mn_3(PO_4)_2$ are sparingly soluble.
OH^-	All *hydroxides* are insoluble except for $Ba(OH)_2$, $Ca(OH)_2$, AuOH, LiOH, NaOH, KOH, and $Sr(OH)_2$. The compounds $Pb(OH)_2$, $Ni(OH)_2$, and $Sn(OH)_4$, are sparingly soluble.
S^{2-}	All *sulfides* are insoluble except for $(NH_4)_2S$, Na_2S, K_2S, and SrS. The compound CaS is sparingly soluble.

HUMBERSIDE COLLEGIATE INSTITUTE

NUMBER .... C27/84 ....

You are given the use of this book on the under-
standing that you will use it with care. Do not mark
it in any way, since another student will use it next
year. Return it next June in good condition or you
will be required to replace it.

NAME ....

FORM..........YEAR ....TEACHER ....

NAME ....

FORM..........YEAR ....TEACHER ....

NAME ....

FORM..........YEAR ....TEACHER ....

NAME ....

FORM..........YEAR ....TEACHER ....

Name	Symbol	Number	Mass
Erbium	Er	68	167.3
Europium	Eu	63	152.0
Fermium	Fm	100	(253)
Fluorine	F	9	19.0
Francium	Fr	87	(223)
Gadolinium	Gd	64	157.2
Gallium	Ga	31	69.7
Germanium	Ge	32	72.6
Gold	Au	79	197.0
Hafnium	Hf	72	178.5
Helium	He	2	4.00
Holmium	Ho	67	164.9
Hydrogen	H	1	1.008
Indium	In	49	114.8
Iodine	I	53	126.9
Iridium	Ir	77	192.2
Iron	Fe	26	55.8
Krypton	Kr	36	83.8
Lanthanum	La	57	138.9
Lawrencium	Lr	103	(256)
Lead	Pb	82	207.2
Lithium	Li	3	6.94
Lutetium	Lu	71	175.0
Magnesium	Mg	12	24.3
Manganese	Mn	25	54.9
Mendelevium	Md	101	(257)
Mercury	Hg	80	200.6

*A value given in parentheses denotes the mass of the isotope with the longest known half-life.

Name	Symbol	Number	Mass
Scandium	Sc	21	45.0
Selenium	Se	34	79.0
Silicon	Si	14	28.1
Silver	Ag	47	107.9
Sodium	Na	11	23.0
Strontium	Sr	38	87.6
Sulfur	S	16	32.1
Tantalum	Ta	73	180.9
Technetium	Tc	43	(97)
Tellurium	Te	52	127.6
Terbium	Tb	65	158.9
Thallium	Tl	81	204.4
Thorium	Th	90	232.0
Thulium	Tm	69	168.9
Tin	Sn	50	118.7
Titanium	Ti	22	47.9
Tungsten (Wolfram)	W	74	183.8
Uranium	U	92	238.0
Vanadium	V	23	50.9
Xenon	Xe	54	131.3
Ytterbium	Yb	70	173.0
Yttrium	Y	39	88.9
Zinc	Zn	30	65.4
Zirconium	Zr	40	91.2
—	—	104**	(260)
—	—	105	(262)

**The names and symbols of elements 104 and 105 have not yet been agreed upon internationally